Courageous
Compassion

Courageous Compassion

A Prophetic Homiletic in Service to the Church

Jerry Taylor
edited by David Fleer

Abilene Christian University Press

COURAGEOUS COMPASSION
A Prophetic Homiletic in Service to the Church

Copyright 2011 by Jerry Taylor

First edition

ISBN 978-0-89112-545-7

LCCN 2010048580

Printed in the United States of America

ALL RIGHTS RESERVED

No part of this publication may be reproduced, stored in a retrieval system, or transmitted in any form by any means—electronic, mechanical, photocopying, recording or otherwise—without prior written consent.

Scripture quotations, unless otherwise noted, are from The Holy Bible, New International Version. Copyright 1984, International Bible Society. Used by permission of Zondervan Publishers.

LIBRARY OF CONGRESS CATALOGING-IN-PUBLICATION DATA
Taylor, Jerry, 1961-
 Courageous compassion : a prophetic homiletic in service to the church / Jerry Taylor ; David Fleer, editor. -- 1st ed.
    p. cm.
 ISBN 978-0-89112-545-7
 1. Sermons, American--African American authors. 2. Sermons, American--21st century. 3. Churches of Christ--Sermons. I. Fleer, David. II. Title. III. Title: Prophetic homiletic in service to the church.
 BV4253.T395 2010
 252'.0663--dc22

                                                                    2010048580

Cover design by Jennette Munger
Interior text design by Sandy Armstrong

For information contact:
Abilene Christian University Press
1626 Campus Court
Abilene, Texas 79601

1-877-816-4455
www.abilenechristianuniversitypress.com

10 11 12 13 14 15 / 7 6 5 4 3 2 1

Dedication

I dedicate this book to Pat, Alisha, and Jeremiah, my wife and children who have been so understanding of the ministry demands on my time. Pat has been a loving support to me and my preaching ministry. Her strength of character, patience, and care for our family have been exemplary. She has also been consistent in helping to instill in our children a desire for a world that is filled with compassion, justice, and peace.

I also dedicate the book to my mother, Alma Hines, and my stepfather, J. B. Hines Jr. (deceased). My mother prayed for me while she carried me in her womb that God would one day let me grow up to be a preacher. My stepfather modeled for me an unrelenting spirit of courage in the face of injustice.

Finally, I dedicate this book to Mrs. Merrel Durham my ninth-grade English teacher at Millington Central High School in Millington, Tennessee. Upon hearing that I had preached my first sermon, Mrs. Durham, a white female, asked me to deliver a sermon in her class. I spoke on racial equality. In response to my sermon she wrote me an inspiring letter that since that day has encouraged me in the pursuit of education and in the carrying out of my preaching vocation.

CONTENTS

	INTRODUCTION	9
	David Fleer: A Prophetic Word for Our Times	9
1	TWO HOUSES IN A STORM	25
	Jerry Taylor: Compositional Notes	25
	Jerry Taylor's Sermon: Two Houses in a Storm	26
	Gary Selby: A Rhetorical Critical Response to "Two Houses in a Storm"	34
2	SONG OF THE VINEYARD	51
	Jerry Taylor: Compositional Notes	51
	Jerry Taylor's Sermon: The Song of the Vineyard	53
	Walter Brueggemann: A Critical Biblical Response to "The Song of the Vineyard"	62
3	WHAT DOES THE LORD REQUIRE?	65
	Jerry Taylor: Compositional Notes	65
	Jerry Taylor's Sermon: What Does the Lord Require?	67
	Walter Bruggemann: A Critical Biblical Response to "What Does the Lord Require?"	78
4	THE LEGACY OF QUEEN VASHTI	81
	Jerry Taylor: Compositional Notes	81
	Jerry Taylor's Sermon: The Legacy of Queen Vashti	83
	Ron Allen: A Theological and Homiletical Response to "The Legacy of Queen Vashti"	92
5	CHRISTMAS ACCORDING TO MATTHEW	95
	Jerry Taylor: Compositional Notes	95
	Jerry Taylor's Sermon: Christmas According to Matthew	97
	Hubert G. Locke: What is a Sermon in the African American Tradition in Churches of Christ?	103

6	BEING STILL IN GOD'S MOVEMENT	107
	Jerry Taylor: Compositional Notes	107
	Jerry Taylor's Sermon: Being Still in God's Movement	108
	Frank A. Thomas: Taylor's Preaching in the Tradition of John the Baptist	120
7	THE VENTRILOQUIST	123
	Jerry Taylor: Compositional Notes	123
	Jerry Taylor's Sermon: The Ventriloquist	124
	David Faust: An Evangelical Reflection on "The Ventriloquist"	130
8	COURAGEOUS COMPASSION	133
	Jerry Taylor: Compositional Notes	133
	Jerry Taylor's Sermon: Courageous Compassion	134
9	THE SPIRIT OF INDEPENDENCE	141
	Jerry Taylor: Compositional Notes	141
	Jerry Taylor's Sermon: The Spirit of Independence	143

Introduction

A Prophetic Word for Our Times

David Fleer

I write this on June 19, an important day in the history of freedom and justice in the United States. On this day in 1862 the U.S. Congress outlawed slavery in United States territories, nullifying the Dred Scott case which prohibited blacks from citizenship. However, in the throes of the Civil War, Confederate states were not accepting new laws from Washington, and freedom was forced to wait.

Exactly three years later, on June 19, 1865, two thousand troops arrived by ship in Galveston, Texas, where Major General Gordon Granger stood on the balcony of the Ashton Villa to announce that the Emancipation Proclamation would be enforced by military means. The remaining slaves in the nation were proclaimed liberated: "The rumors they had heard were indeed true. The Civil War had ended and they were now free."[1]

However, as the following century passed, progress for racial justice and real freedom moved painfully slow. Thus, on June 19, 1963,

President John Kennedy sent a draft of the civil rights bill to Congress. He concluded this message:

> I ask you to look into your hearts—not in search of charity, for the Negro neither wants nor needs condescension—but for the one plain, proud and priceless quality that united us all as Americans: A sense of justice. In this year of the emancipation centennial, justice requires us to insure the blessings of liberty for all Americans and their posterity—not merely for reasons of economic efficiency, world diplomacy and domestic tranquility—but, above all, because it is right.[2]

One year after Kennedy called upon Congress to transcend economic and diplomatic reasons to address the morality of justice—on June 19, 1964—the U.S. Senate passed the Civil Rights Bill, banning segregation in schools, businesses, and places of interstate commerce. The bill was quite specific, listing public venues where segregation was forbidden including restaurants, lunch counters, soda fountains, gasoline stations, hotels, motels, and theatres.

Nearly a half century later, however, what most surprises is not the bill's detailed listing of specific public venues, but that the bill's passage followed an eighty-three-day Senate filibuster. The reality of a staunch, vocal, and articulate resistance to racial justice disturbs and shares a symbolic connection to June 19.

On June 19, 1964, Senator Richard B. Russell, Democrat of Georgia and leader of the Southern opposition, angrily denounced the press, clergy, and unions who had exerted pressure on Congress to pass what he called an "unconstitutional" bill, destructive of the system of divided powers and states' rights, and directed solely at the South.[3]

On the same day West Virginia Senator Robert Byrd defended his vote against the bill by saying that the measure "goes beyond" equal justice and provides "special treatment" for some people. In doing so, it "does violence to long-established constitutional principles."

On the same day New Mexico Senator Edwin L. Mechem voted against the bill because the sections on fair employment and public accommodations "could assure the greatest assault on property ownership and private enterprise this country has known."

On that same day Senator George A. Smathers, Democrat of Florida, complained "we find all of the force of the Federal Government directed at the South" and predicted that if a dictator ever appeared in this country, "that man will ride to power on the influence . . . he will get under Titles VI and VII."

On June 19, 1964, states' rights, constitutional principles, property concerns, and Southern offense framed the core of the argument for resistance to civil rights. Even more disturbing, the names and political history of the vocal opposition reveal that the resisters had not emerged from society's fringes. In fact, the most visible Senate opponent, Arizona's Barry Goldwater, had enough political clout that year to capture the Republican nomination for U.S. President. The battle for justice was hard fought because resistance was so deeply and strategically entrenched.

After the bill's June 19 passage, in an effort to assuage his fellow lawmakers of the rancor and bitterness of debate, Minnesota Senator Hubert Humphrey appealed to the prophetic language of Scripture and called Congress to a higher ideal: "We are engaged in the age-old struggle within all men—a struggle to overcome irrational legacies, a struggle to escape the bondage of ignorance and poverty, a struggle to create a new and better community where 'justice rolls down like waters and righteous[-ness, like] a mighty stream.'"[4]

So, June 19 is a significant day to pen an introduction to a volume that reflects on social justice, the prophetic call, the reality of resistance, and the need for courageous compassion. When the struggle is long and opposition well funded and passionately held, how does one effectively speak truth to power? How does one achieve the balance of justice and kindness in a humble walk with the Lord? June 19 is a perfect day to consider the prophetic preaching of Jerry Taylor, an African American minister in the Churches of Christ who serves as Assistant Professor of Bible, Missions and Ministry at Abilene Christian University.

Jerry Taylor now teaches at an institution that one-half century ago was a bastion of civil rights repression and social injustice against African Americans. Then, in early 1960, a watershed moment occurred during the Abilene Christian College Bible Lectureship. Under the theme "Christian Faith in the Modern World," ACC Professor Carl Spain spoke prophetically against entrenched institutional racism. Born in Chattanooga, Tennessee and raised in Alabama and Georgia, the forty-three-year-old preacher and Bible professor asked, "Are we moral cowards on this issue? There are people with money who will back us in our last ditch stand for white supremacy in a world of pigmented people. God forbid that we shall be the last stronghold among religious schools where the politico-economic philosophy of naturalism determines our moral conduct."[5] In his speech Spain creatively cast Jesus as a prophet and challenged the college's administration and church leaders: "Ye hypocrites! You say you are the only true Christians, and make up the only true church, and have the only Christian schools. Yet, you drive one of your own preachers to denominational schools where he can get credit for his work and refuse to let him take Bible for credit ... because the color of his skin is dark!"[6]

For the nation at large desegregation was aided by the "bully pulpit" of congressional legislation and enhanced with the promise of financial rewards, which in the 1960s eventually prompted southern public universities to comply with the law.[7] In sharp contrast, Carl Spain's singular appeal was to moral authority. As President Kennedy would urge Congress three years later, Spain claimed that social change should occur, not for economic efficiency or domestic tranquility, but "because it is *right*."

With the passing of years, Spain's speech has been elevated to prophetic status in the Churches of Christ. It is oft proclaimed that his oration evoked such strong support that Abilene Christian College began admitting black students to its graduate programs twenty months after the speech and undergraduate black students began to matriculate in 1962.[8] So, in one sense, it is appropriate to say that Jerry Taylor stands today on the prophetic shoulders of Carl Spain.

Moreover, Spain's speech signified the beginning of a prophetic evolution transpiring at Abilene Christian College and throughout the country. For example, Robert Byrd, the segregationist West Virginia Democrat who voted against Civil Rights legislation and had been a member of the Ku Klux Klan, came to repudiate his past actions. During a pivotal point in the 2008 Presidential Primary he endorsed and campaigned for the election of Barack Obama, whom he labeled, "A noble-hearted patriot and humble Christian [who] has my full faith and support."[9] The complete shift had taken a life time: the former segregationist supported an African American for president.

Abilene Christian University and the religious fellowship it represents have evolved as well. A decade ago ACU President Royce Money issued a public apology, confessing the university's "sins of racism and discrimination."[10] The apology was presented during the fiftieth anniversary Founders' Day celebration at Southwestern Christian College in Terrell, Texas, a predominately African American institution established because African Americans were excluded from ACU and most other colleges associated with the Churches of Christ. Jerry Taylor's ACU faculty position provides additional evidence of the university's shift in policy over the last half century.

In the long evolution of civil rights and social justice, resistance and tension ran especially high in the 1960s. The Civil Rights Movement received hearty engagements from opposing sides. Legislation supported by the president and passed in Congress provided stark contrast to the filibustering senators and the racism embedded at ACC which Carl Spain opposed—a contrast revealing that white Churches of Christ firmly stood within the "Southern opposition" articulated by Robert

Byrd, Richard Russell, and their segregationist colleagues. Religion, in this case, argued for separation of church and state, extricating social action from Christian doctrine, believing the "social gospel" antithetical to "the Gospel of Jesus Christ."[11]

But evolution does not occur on a clear and faultless track and history reveals flaws in heroes and heroic moments. For example, when Carl Spain's speech is viewed through the lens of its larger context and the "prophet's" response to critique, a more nuanced and less pristine moment surfaces.

The biting indictments in Spain's speech are framed by a context of restraint. Spain prefaced his rebuke by clarifying that he did *not* support impending Civil Rights legislation: "In correcting social evils, we must resort to the educational approach before we attempt legislation."[12] Then, Spain immediately qualified his strong prophetic language with specific parameters for opening the college to African American students: "Brethren, we are not recommending revolutionary legislation . . . . If the problem is one of room and board, then let us consider that we have no problem if we do not have to provide room and board."[13] The speech's prophetic sting is assuaged by the compromised context of legislative opposition and "integration restrictions" that would have kept black students out of the dormitories and off campus "after hours."

Even more telling are the marginal comments written in the used volume I obtained less than two decades after the event. The lectureship book was published in early February and available to conferees at the 1960 event. In the copy I now possess, penned in tight cursive script, one auditor judged, "[Spain's] argument was well received by those who heard it, but it remains to be seen how well they act upon their outward show of approval." The comments are dated February 25, 1960 and add this revealing notation: "Bro. Spain has been challenged by a preacher of the church in the past 24 hours to debate this question. Bro. Spain said he would only preach it and his preacher friend could preach what he believed."[14]

Spain's compromise surfaces essential questions. Must prophetic speech be couched in concession to gain a hearing? How does one implement prophetic rhetoric? How does a prophet exhibit courageous compassion?

Some say that the evolution is now complete; that the Civil Rights Movement belongs to the confines of a chapter in a history book; that those under a certain age are no longer caught up in the struggles of the past.

"Times have changed," they say. "Look how far we have advanced."

They admit, "Folks aged over sixty may still harbor racial insensitivities," but argue, "younger Americans are radically different."

They confess, "We acknowledge a difficult past," but claim, "everything changed on a particular day long ago (June 19)," and therefore plead, "Let bygones be bygones." Members of the Churches of Christ like to believe that Carl Spain's 1960 lectureship address was their "continental divide."

But, we should not be too quick to declare that the evolution toward social justice is finished. Racism, as Cornell West somewhere said, didn't die with the Civil Rights Movement; it remained vibrantly alive and thrived "underground." The truth is: systemic injustice is not easily uprooted especially in a Christian community where the dichotomy of social action and doctrine continue to run deep and the "social gospel" is considered antithetical to "the Gospel of Jesus Christ."

One recent spring Sunday I drove to church wondering if that morning's news might somehow appear in the sermon, if church could meaningfully connect with world affairs. The issues at stake were different expressions of disturbing social violence erupting around the globe. So, I wondered if while gathered with the community of believers we would be asked to ignore "social issues" or if church would be perceived as the place where we might process the events of the day. Would church pretend social turmoil didn't exist or find some means of interpretation? Would we again hear, "Don't take sides or get involved in political matters"? Or might this Sunday provide some theological foundation for living in these politically violent days?

That morning's Internet news feeds reported the latest outbreaks of brutal violence in the Congo, where nearly seven million have been killed during the last dozen years. Rape, torture, and mutilation were described in horrific detail, and I was tempted to look the other way, dismiss the images, and avoid the heartache and pain. Without thoughtful engagement, news of the atrocities was too much to bear.

Must church nurture the desire to hide? *Can* church provide appropriate insight on these difficult realities? *Will* church address social upheaval on the world stage with theological sensitivity and meaningful reflection?

That morning's news also continued conversations surrounding the seething debate over U.S. healthcare, which had produced venomous slurs hurled at John Lewis and other African American congressmen. During the week reports of death threats and vandalism stretched from Arizona to upstate New York, as F.B.I. and local police were enlisted to protect members of Congress and their families.

Would these national events be mentioned in the pulpit? Would the sermon address causes and expressions of racism and hatred? Would the preacher challenge the common wisdom that hatred inevitably accelerates and that war ends war? Or, might the preacher instead cast a biblical vision for a radically different way to understand and live in this world?

Earlier in the month Fox News personality Glenn Beck set out to convince his audience that the term "social justice" is "code" for communism and Nazism. Beck urged Christians to discuss the term with their pastors and priests and to leave their churches if leaders would not reconsider their emphasis on social justice. On his radio program, Beck declared, "I beg you, look for the words 'social justice' or 'economic justice' on your church Web site. If you find it, run as fast as you can. Social justice and economic justice, they are code words. Now, am I advising people to leave their church? Yes."[15]

I wondered what kind of impact Glenn Beck was having on my brothers and sisters at the predominately white congregation that I would attend that Sunday morning, knowing from prior conversations that many were avid listeners. And I worried—given the fierce anger and divisive discourse currently raging on the airwaves and at political rallies—whose values might orient the sermon, the conversations around the communion table, and the casual exchanges before and after the service.

On the drive to church that spring morning I was troubled by the likely dissociation I would face. The source of my troubles were the biblical emphases and declarations of God's concerns; because social justice is very much embedded in Scripture, from Jesus' inaugural sermon[16] to the description of the early Christian community modeled after him: "For there was not a needy person among them, for all who owned land or houses sold them and brought the proceeds of the sales and lay them at the apostles' feet, and it was distributed to each as any had need."[17] When rich and powerful people asked how they could be part of the Kingdom of God, Jesus advised, "sell what you own, and give the money to the poor, and you will have treasure in heaven; then come, follow me." I was troubled because I *need* church to keep me from turning away, to remind me of the seriousness of Scripture's claims, to help me address the persistent outcroppings of social oppression.

In a Christian fellowship with a history of separating social action from a privatized gospel of conversion and amidst current popular voices of resistance, such preaching is hard to find. Where in the Churches of Christ might such a voice be found? Prophets are rare and truth telling has its price. Where are today's Christian models of courageous compassion?

Over the last two decades such a voice has emerged with remarkable rhetorical power and biblical depth. Jerry Taylor is an effective preacher in the Churches of Christ and other segments of the Stone Campbell Movement. He has recently keynoted its major lectureships and church venues. His abilities have drawn the attention of those outside his denomination and in 2006 he delivered the plenary address for the North American Christian Convention. His preaching is characterized as a "compassionate prophetic voice" delivered in the traditional African American form: "Start slow, stay low, rise higher, and end in fire." His preaching is intelligent and wedded to the biblical text which effectively engages listeners before it explodes with persuasion. He creates from Scripture deep and alternative worlds, exhibiting a respect for God and God's kingdom which invites listeners to find lasting wisdom and life altering perspectives through a biblical vision.

To begin this volume's assessment of Taylor's work we address listeners' initial response to a Taylor sermon—"That was powerful! How did that happen?"—through his sermon, "Two Houses in a Storm," delivered at the closing plenary for the Pepperdine Bible Lectures in May, 2008. Rhetorical critic and Civil Rights advocate, Gary Selby, probes the sermon to discover how it works so well. His systematic and scholarly rhetorical assessment explains how Taylor's sermon embodies the biblical model of *parrhesia* ("candid speech that unsettles folk from sleep walking") which works in such a way that Taylor has no need to *directly* exhort his hearers to embrace the function of the biblical text, because "by the sermon's conclusion, they have boldly taken that stand on their own." While times have changed and significant advances toward racial and social justice have been made, Selby's examination shows how Taylor advances the conversation even with those who may instinctively resist the subject. Selby thus reveals how the provocative work of Taylor's prophetic preaching is not couched in compromise to gain a hearing, but exhibits courageous compassion, helping the church address social upheaval on the world stage with theological sensitivity and meaningful reflection.

When President Kennedy introduced his Civil Rights legislation in 1963, he built his plea for passage upon an essential assumption: that members of congress, clearly conversant with the language of economic efficiency, world diplomacy, and domestic tranquility, would also have the moral capacity to understand what was *"right."* The prophetic preacher, however, cannot assume moral clarity, but must define from paradigmatic biblical narratives the weightier matters, the greatest commandments, and those issues "of first importance."[18] In other words, the prophetic preacher trades not in biblical sound bites, but the most essential qualities underscored in Scripture. Jerry Taylor's courage to turn to the world of Scripture with compassionate understanding sets him apart from the standard "voices" that fill the air . . . and justifies a volume that assesses the strength of his work.

Therefore, the second and third chapters in this volume include the sermons, "Song of the Vineyard" and "What Does the Lord Require?" and fall under the careful scrutiny of Old Testament scholar, Walter Brueggemann, whose career has been spent examining prophetic literature in such works as *David's Truth in Israel's Imagination and Memory* and *The Prophetic Imagination*. Brueggemann, known for his ability to combine literary and sociological methods to create a post-liberal analysis of Scripture, shows how Taylor engages the world envisioned in the text and explores the ways Taylor's preaching focuses on the primary accent points in Isaiah 5 and Micah 6. Brueggemann's critique helps us bring clarity to the specific places where Taylor's sermon lingers long over the particularities of these texts and assures us *whose values* orient these sermons.

Homiletician and biblical scholar Ron Allen provides both homiletic and theological insight into Taylor's fourth sermon in the collection, "The Legacy of Queen Vashti." Allen begins by dismissing the popular definition of prophetic speech as "angry confrontation" and recasts the prophet as a kind of ombudsperson, a person who helps the community consider how they are living in accord with God's purposes. The prophet helps the community recognize unfaithfulness in order to take action, providing a theological foundation for living in these politically charged days. Allen finds "The Legacy of Queen Vashti" homiletically instructive and a model for prophetic preaching, even from parts of the Bible not technically in the prophetic corpu.

Taylor's fifth sermon in the collection, "Christmas According to Matthew," is cause for Hubert Locke's reflective essay, "What Is a Sermon in the African American Tradition in Churches of Christ?" Locke, whose distinguished theological and academic career has been centered on justice in society, preached in Detroit throughout the 1960s. Locke commends Taylor's "sermonic prowess," accenting the sermon's remarkable shift away from traditions of sectarianism and restricted sermonic function. He reveals how "Christmas According to Matthew" is a fine example of the kind of biblical preaching which stands at the core of a healthy heritage in Churches of Christ, a heritage founded on the conviction that the Bible is the Word of God. Locke thus identifies within Churches of Christ a prophetic, truth telling voice capable of casting a biblical vision for a radically different way to understand and live in this world.

The following chapter expands and sharpens the critique of Taylor's work with a focus on the "courageous" side of his preaching. Frank Thomas, senior pastor of Mississippi Boulevard Baptist Church in Memphis and author of *They Like to Never Quit Praisin' God: The Role of Celebration in Preaching*, evaluates Taylor's work from the larger vantage of prophetic preaching and the African American pulpit. For his assessment, Thomas turns to John the Baptist for a clear and specific standard for prophetic preaching. John the Baptist's model exhibits an allegiance to God's domain, calls into question the present religious and political system, and challenges the ruling class. Upon this specific standard, Thomas judges that Taylor's sermon, "Being Still in God's Movement," firmly stands in the prophetic tradition of John the Baptist and presents an excellent model of contemporary prophetic preaching capable of addressing international events and identifying causes and expressions of hatred and racism. Staunch, vocal, and articulate resistance to social justice continues to emerge—and not from society's fringes—with enough political clout to continue to capture regional and national elections. The battle for social justice continues because resistance remains so deeply and strategically entrenched and demands the foundation of biblical perspectives and the courage of John the Baptist.

"The Ventriloquist" provides a most unique engagement opportunity. Delivered to an exclusively African American audience, the sermon is evaluated from an Evangelical vantage point. David Faust, president of Cincinnati Christian University, provides a traditional Evangelical critique, judging Taylor's work by these standards: Is the sermon biblical? Is it Christ-centered? Does it build faith, hope, and love? I ask you, the reader, to push forward Faust's assessments. Specifically, if we embrace Christ and the cross, is that not all the more reason to preach social justice? On the other hand, I encourage you to challenge the Evangelical presuppositions. Ask: what makes a sermon biblical? Must a sermon include the cross when the text does not? Must every sermon fit the agenda of building faith, hope, and love? Or, might the focus and function of a particular text impact the focus and function of the sermon? Most important, I ask you to question the presupposition about *how* the sermon connects with audience needs. "Good preaching," Faust claims, "should meet the listener's deepest needs," which he explains to mean, "evangelize, bringing good news to those who need a faith lift and an infusion of hope." Faust's critique is clear and honest, but limits its focus to the individual. The individual construct is foreign to many texts where a *community* of believers is addressed, including "The Ventriloquist" from Acts 16. This kind of critical and interactive dialogue can enhance your reading of this sermon and the body of Taylor's work.

The volume comes full circle in the final two chapters and with the two audio sermons available inside the back cover. As Gary Selby's critique underscores, full appreciation of Jerry Taylor's homiletic depth is not complete without attention to his delivery. The audio version of "Two Houses in a Storm" provides opportunity to better engage and judge Selby's assessment. The audio version of the "Fourth of July Address" provides another opportunity to hear Taylor's delivery and, coupled with the final chapter, "Courageous Compassion," allows listeners and readers to further develop their own critical review of Taylor's work, using some of the biblical, rhetorical, theological, and homiletic tools displayed in the volume.

Social, gender, sexual, and racial tensions persist today among all ages and classes. This tension is especially exposed when preaching proposes that prophetic biblical texts are read with our particular situations in mind; especially when prophetic preaching seeks to recapture the biblical themes and images that our churches have forgotten; especially when preaching breaks with the distorted notion of a Christianity which dismisses Scripture's paradigmatic social concerns.

"Let justice roll down like waters and righteousness like an ever-flowing stream,"[19] Hubert Humphrey quoted—*after* the favorable vote for Civil Rights, borrowing his eighth-century prophetic text from the manuscript of Civil Rights leaders and applying it to internecine congressional disgruntlement. The text, as Humphrey used it, didn't aid the community's wisdom and ability to craft appropriate legislation. Taylor's work, in stark contrast, intends to shape communities willing to enter with him into the realities envisioned within the paradigmatic prophetic narratives in Scripture.

In Scripture, from the Prophets to the Gospels, the people of God are consistently called to embody social justice, often against the resisting powers of the empire. In an ironic turn, our recent experience has forced the powers of the world to provide the people of God example and motivation to embody social justice.[20] The church's evolution toward social justice has not been swift, nor is it complete. The struggle continues and opposition remains volatile and articulate. In this context, Taylor shows that prophetic speech need not be couched in compromise to gain a hearing. Instead, he effectively models how to speak truth to power by achieving a balance of justice and kindness—a "courageous compassion." Taylor provides listeners and readers an insightful foundation for living in these politically charged days by engaging national events and identifying the causes and expressions of racism and hatred. He appropriately challenges the common wisdom of our culture by articulating a biblical vision that opens our eyes to live into the realities God intends for us.

1

Two Houses in a Storm

Compositional Notes

This message was delivered on May 2, 2008 at the Pepperdine University Lectureship in Malibu, California. The majority white audience was both politically and religiously conservative. As I developed the sermon I experienced an intense internal struggle between a desire to be a popular preacher and the calling to be a prophetic voice. The sermon was developed during the height of the historic presidential campaign of 2008. Barack Obama had become the first African American to be nominated by a major political party in America to run for president of the United States. Then Senator Obama's race for the oval office brought race and racial tension in this country to the forefront of the American mind.

With the national climate of racism growing hot and humid, I sensed the urgency to plead with the followers of the Sermon on the

Mount to be peacemakers in the face of the approaching political, economic, and social storm. The immediate social crisis we faced as a nation in the spring of 2008, along with the hateful rhetoric that spewed from the mouths of talk show hosts and political pundits, made the moment pregnant with the potential for violent strife.

After putting the finishing touches on the sermon, I vividly remember the night prior to delivering the message standing in quiet contemplation in the Heroes Garden. Heroes Garden is a memorial on the Pepperdine University campus dedicated to the lives that perished in the attacks on the World Trade Center in New York City on September 11, 2001. As I stood in the Heroes Garden overlooking the Pacific Ocean, I was reminded that this was a very serious time that demanded an earnest expression and recollection of an age-old truth that Jesus delivered in the Sermon on the Mount nearly two thousand years ago. I figured in a modern world that is often given over to the maddening insanity of war and racial hatred, it would be a truth difficult to receive.

TWO HOUSES IN A STORM

Matthew 7:24-29

Jesus concludes the Sermon on the Mount by using a parable that confronts us with two choices. Once we hear the words of Jesus, we can either choose to put them into practice, thus being like a wise builder who builds his house upon a rock, or we can choose not to put them into practice, thus being like a foolish builder who builds his house upon sand. Each choice will be thoroughly tested. According to the parable, both houses will face harsh weather conditions. How well each construction holds up during severe weather will be determined by the strength or weakness of its foundation. It is during severe crisis when the limits of a foundation are fully revealed. Therefore, a life constructed on the words of Jesus will withstand the full blast of a category five storm, but a life constructed on the words and opinions of humans will face total ruin in the midst of the same tempest. For this reason, the words of Jesus are more essential than all other words spoken in the world.

The world is filled with words. On the one hand, it is filled with graceful words that make peace as well as with angry words that make war. Words are boxcars in the train of thought that often carry toxic energy into the public square. The words of Jesus, if communicated correctly, have the capacity to move the world towards a healthy humanity. On the other hand, words that do not belong to Jesus are often used as weapons of mass deceit that covertly coerce people into practices that conflict with Jesus' Sermon on the Mount.

The Genesis account of creation shows that God is the first communicator. However, just as God speaks creative words, Satan follows by speaking words contaminated with evil intent. It is satanic speech making that disrupts the harmony of society in the Garden of Eden. Since Satan's first speech to Adam and Eve, his public speaking career has soared to the heights of smashing success. Not only does Satan display the ability to use his own words to undermine the words of God, he also demonstrates the artistic ability of a ventriloquist. In Genesis, Satan makes his first speech through the mouth of a snake. Since the Garden of Eden, Satan has upgraded his tactic from speaking his words through a single snake to conveying his agenda through an entire den of serpents. Satan pulls the strings that move the mouths of public serpents. He is the chief speechwriter, who puts his lying words into speeches that mislead unsuspecting loyalists to support brutal activities that ruthlessly strike against the cheek of the Sermon on the Mount.

In the Old Testament, these public serpents are called false prophets. False prophets speak deceitful words that lead to what Walter Brueggemann calls a "false consciousness." Deceptive and misleading words spoken by false prophets are the greatest threat to the public safety and social harmony of any society. Samuel Johnson once said, "Do not lie to one another, since the society of Hell could not subsist without truth any more than others." Albert Camus says, "We have a right to think that truth with a capital letter is relative. But facts are facts. And whoever says that the sky is blue when it is gray is prostituting words and preparing the way for tyranny."

As a Christian, I believe that the truthful words of Jesus activated in the lives of Christians are essential to the peaceful longevity of stability in any society. In the broader literary context of Matthew 7, Jesus makes it clear that false prophets are the greatest threat to people hearing and putting his words into practice. Jesus says in Matthew 7:15, "Watch out for false prophets. They come to you in sheep's clothing, but inwardly they are ferocious wolves. By their fruit you will recognize them." False prophets have a peaceful exterior, but their inner nature is a swirling chaos of violence moving about like a tornado looking for a place to touch down. They are grievous wolves that spare not the flock. They are greedy for power, gain, and self-promotion by any means necessary.

False prophets seek to convince the disciples of Jesus that the Sermon on the Mount is impractical in the real world. However, false prophets do see some value in the words of Jesus. They see his words as valuable commodities to be sold for profit in the marketplace of religious consumerism. Jesus knew that false prophets would always be in demand. False prophets have a market that will never suffer a slow down or recession, because religious consumers tirelessly shop for doctrines of ease. They go from church to church like going from yard sale to yard sale, eagerly looking for smooth words that are for sale. They are shopping for words with smooth edges that will calm the feelings of guilt that arise when they intentionally choose not to put into practice the words of Jesus. They bargain hunt for words that give them permission to seek the destruction of not only their actual persecutors, but also the obliteration of anyone who could potentially pose a threat of persecuting them in the future. They want modern prophets, who will tell them that they don't have to endure persecution like the prophets of old, and that they never have to suffer insult by others who spread false propaganda by saying all kinds of evil against them for Jesus' sake.

Religious consumers want theologians to serve as constantinian apologists in order to prove that Jesus endorses using an earthly government to protect Christians from any potential threat of religious persecution. Religious consumers want to buy the services of the theologically trained that can prove, by human logic, that good cannot overcome evil and that Satan actually can cast out Satan by the mutual exercise of evil on both sides. Christian consumers seek to purchase the intellectual services of academic soothsayers, who give them ethical sanction to desire leaders who refuse to let their yes be yes and their no be no. These leaders are willing to lie, deceive, mislead, and distort the truth when it is believed to be done in order to protect and preserve the interest of our group, be it race, religion, corporation, or nation. Religious consumers are scouting for the skilled wordsmith who gives them moral permission to store up treasures on earth in barns that grow bigger in each economic growth cycle, while they watch with apathetic indifference a bleeding and hungry Lazarus begging for mercy on their security cameras at the entrance to their beautifully adorned security gates. Christian consumers continue to worship at the altar of mammon as they watch and listen to televised preachers standing on the prosperity platform, teaching Christians that it is possible to serve both God and money. They shop for rainy words that water down the message of the Sermon on the Mount with such saturation that it causes moral mudslides in the lives of Christians, leaving them unprepared to respond nonviolently to the presence of evil in our world today.

Cultural Christianity has subliminally conditioned Christians to be willing to hate and kill their enemies without mercy when it is deemed necessary. In this very critical hour in human history, I am afraid that many Christians have exchanged their "kingdom consciousness" for a "cultural consciousness." Their foundations are no longer the words of Jesus but instead are the words of men. However, the truth remains that, whatever the foundation is, it is going to be thoroughly tested. The final judgment is not the only time when the foundations of our well-constructed lives will experience adversity. The foundations of our lives will also be tried during periods of intense human conflict, social strife, civil unrest, and international power struggles that unfold across the aging face of this tired planet. Unless Christians remain radically committed to living the Sermon on the Mount in this nation, we will have no way of storm-proofing our society against the dark social clouds that are gathering on yonder horizon.

Hearing and witnessing the televised violent and bloody clashes between warring factions in third-world countries ought to help us see all the more clearly the need for Christians to sincerely embody and live out Jesus' teachings in the Sermon on the Mount within the context of our own nation. If the hour should ever return in this nation when civil struggle turns overtly violent, I pray there will be enough Christians left in this country who still believe in Jesus' message of nonviolence. I pray that Christians will be prepared to serve as stabilizing salt in the midst of a nation growing tired and weary of words that express superficial politeness in the pretentious guise of political correctness.

If you have watched television or listened to the radio during the present political season, you will have seen evidence that our nation is possibly sliding in the dangerous direction of social conflict. The airwaves of this nation are being filled not with the words of Jesus, but with the toxic words of anger. More and more people in this country are being recruited to build their lives upon the unreliable quicksand of anger, rage, hostility, bitterness, and vindictive retaliation. Angry preachers and radio personalities use their public platform as a long-handle spoon to stir vigorously into the raw emotions of human fury. Their enraged words are turning the American melting pot into the American boiling pot. Many Christians are substituting the voice of the chief shepherd for the voices of the mad prophets of the airwaves who are driven by a spirit of anger. Many radio and television personalities have become the dominant pulpits in our society. They are boldly preaching a message that is not inspired by the Holy Spirit and does not embrace the nonviolent values of Jesus Christ. While these pulpits of the airwaves are sounding their message with great volume, many of our pulpits in the churches have become shamefully timid or strangely silent in proclaiming the gospel of peace and reconciliation in regard to race, gender, politics, and religion.

The pulpits in the churches of Jesus Christ must not be intimidated by the influence that livid media personalities possess over the people who sit in the pews on Sunday. Preachers must not be afraid to loudly proclaim from the rooftops that the church of Jesus Christ is built upon the solid foundation of a nonviolent Christ, who is the Prince of Peace. The words of Jesus are so important that they must be spread throughout our nation and throughout the world by those whose beautiful feet are shod with the preparation of the gospel of peace. Our nation and our world cannot afford to go long without hearing the words of Jesus preached, for how shall they hear these words without a preacher, and how shall we preach the words of Jesus with love unless we encounter the God of peace and become intuitively one with his feelings and passions for a wounded and fragmented humanity?

As preachers of the nonviolent Christ, we will lift our voices even if we have to sing a solo of a new song in the face of an angry chorus of voices that insist on singing the same tired song of racial, religious, and political division. As preachers of the words of Jesus, we will no longer practice the violence of silence while watching hate-mongers spread their venomous malice all over this land. We must not be silent while the "war of words" escalates into a "world of war." As preachers of the words of Jesus, we will speak words of truth on behalf of all God's offspring who are suffering in this country and around the world. With humble truth, we will peacefully confront those who seek to ride the "serf" board of greed upon the massive wave of global wealth that is being pushed inland by the high tide of cheap labor.

As preachers of the words of Jesus, we will encourage all Christians to untangle allegiance from institutions that demand the surrender of soul and integrity for the preservation of any kingdom that is of this world. As preachers of the words of Jesus, we will not fight for the right to bear arms, but we will fight for the right of all races and political persuasions to lock arms in peace, therefore together in Christ becoming artisans of peace. While others arm themselves with the carnal weapons of self-defense, we will arm ourselves with the nonviolent weapon, which is the sword of the Spirit, the word of God.

The words in the Sermon on the Mount are meant to be put into practice; his words are not tennis racquets used to volley theological ideas back and forth on the court of scholarly discussion. Too often we have become prisoners of words and are endlessly trapped in meaningless vocabulary. The words of Jesus call us to action. When Jesus calls us, his words do not invite us to take a seat; they invite us to take a stand on the rock of ages. Jesus said "on this rock I will build my church, and the gates of Hades shall not overcome it." As we stand on the rock of truth, we stand on the solid fact that Jesus Christ is the protector and defender of his followers. We do not look to Constantine for security; we look to Christ as our only savior. We stand on Jesus' words by putting them into practice.

Because God's divine nature is in us by the power of the Holy Spirit, we are empowered to put the words of Jesus into practice come hail or high water! Putting the words of Jesus into application is the only way we as Christians will be able to follow the nonviolent Christ in the midst of a world that is in social crisis. Putting the words of Jesus into practice is the only way that we will be empowered to safely wade through the rising waters of social unrest when the floodgates of social conflict are opened. Putting the words of Jesus into practice is the only sure way to weatherize cold hearts and to storm proof our society against the inclement weather that is in the social forecast of hate-mongers.

We will stand on the solid rock when mean-spirited words of false prophets form a severe emotional weather system that moves across this country and world, endangering all expression of spiritual life. We will stand on the solid rock when hateful words from our enemies fall around us like raindrops from a pregnant storm cloud. We will stand on the solid rock when the meteor-sized hail of bitter retaliation leaves huge dents in our desire to forgive those who have trespassed against us. We will stand on the solid rock when the waters of persecutions are rising and Katrina-like winds of rage are blowing against us.

We refuse to stand on the sand of old grudges. We refuse to stand on the sand of rotting wealth. We refuse to stand on the sand of undying anger. We refuse to stand on the shifting and inconstant sand of human popularity that comes from group loyalty. Instead, we have decided to follow Jesus. We will stand on faith, hope, and love, even when our legs are tired and our feet are weary. We will stand on prayer, even when we don't feel like praying for those who spitefully use us and who say all manner of evil about us because of Jesus. We will stand on forgiveness, because we know how much he has forgiven us. Let us stand together, children, to the glory of our Father.

"TWO HOUSES IN A STORM"

A Rhetorical Critical Response

Gary S. Selby

On May 2, 2008, Jerry Taylor stood before a sea of some four thousand mostly white faces gathered in Peppperdine University's Firestone Fieldhouse for the final night of the university's annual Bible Lectures. Taylor's charge was not only to preach on his assigned text, Matthew 7:24-29, but also to bring four days of seminars, workshops, and worship celebrations to their climactic finale. In particular, he was expected to provide a word of exhortation that would bring closure to the series of six keynote addresses on various texts from the Sermon on the Mount that had taken place in the same auditorium over the previous four days. From the outset, Taylor faced an ironic if not an untenable position: to address a passage so radically counter-cultural that even a figure as revolutionary as Martin Luther found himself forced to conclude that its teachings simply could not be applied to a Christian's day-to-day life in the secular world. At the same time, Taylor was expected to send his hearers home feeling warmed and refreshed, a bit closer to God and heaven than when they had come. Indeed, many in his audience planned to cap off the evening's activities with pie and coffee in the school's cafeteria before preparing to return home the next morning. It was no moment for the voice of a prophet—and certainly, not an African American prophet.

And yet, a prophetic word it was. Although Taylor's aim was not immediately obvious when he took the podium, by the end of the sermon his purpose was clear. He hoped to admonish his audience, particularly the leaders of his own Christian tradition, for turning a blind eye and a silent voice to their nation's descent into a culture of militarism. They had ignored or rationalized away what he saw as the Sermon on the Mount's unequivocal demand that Christians live a life of nonviolence. He hoped to awaken his hearers to the danger of complacently accepting the uses of power and force that characterize the institutions of this fallen world. Most of all, he hoped to challenge believers to renew their commitment to practicing the plain teachings of Jesus, who called his followers to love their enemies, turn the other cheek, and even welcome persecution for the sake of the gospel.

Beyond the obvious tensions in his rhetorical situation, Taylor faced two particularly vexing complications as he sought to achieve these aims. First was the status of his audience—middle class and politically moderate to conservative, an audience that arguably enjoyed the easy relationship between church and state that has often characterized Christianity in the United States. Unlike Taylor, who as a black preacher brought with him the Civil Rights Movement's legacy of Christian social activism, his hearers would more nearly have viewed the sacred and secular as separate realms. Their prayer regarding secular society would more nearly have been that they be free to worship "unmolested by the governing authorities." Also complicating his task was the reality that he was a black preacher addressing a predominantly white audience. To be sure, as a black preacher he brought a special ethos to his situation: Who among his white audience would not hear him through the lens of the black church's most famous son and now an American hero, Martin Luther King Jr.? At the same time, that association brought with it the danger that he might be heard merely as a curiosity or worse, as a source for self-congratulation that his religious tradition had moved beyond its own racial history. At the same time, it was inconceivable that his audience could have heard Taylor preach apart from at least some vestige, however subliminal, of their nation's racial history, which visited severe approbation if not violence on African Americans who failed to remain in their "place." In short, Taylor faced the daunting task of bringing a prophetic word to his hearers while navigating between the twin shoals of being dismissed by them on the one hand or alienating them on the other.

He responded to this daunting rhetorical situation by crafting a sermon that ultimately placed his audience in the position of using *parrhesia*—frank, bold, and truthful speech—in order to declare their *own* commitment to what, for Taylor, might best be called "militant nonviolence."[1] In this essay, I highlight two strategic elements of the sermon that played a crucial role in his attempt to bring about this rhetorical aim. First, I show how, across the three moves of the sermon, Taylor creates a complex, evolving set of relationships between himself, his audience, and the outside world that shifts the position of the audience from witnessing his condemnation of the sinful "outside" world, to finding themselves the potential objects of that condemnation, and finally, to becoming participants with him in boldly proclaiming their own fierce determination to stand against violence in their own society.[2] Second, I focus on the way that, in the sermon's third move, Taylor reframes nonviolence as militant action, transforming "turning the other cheek" into "taking a stand" for the truth of the gospel. The result is a symbolic performance, rooted squarely in the black preaching tradition,[3] in which Taylor has no need to directly exhort his hearers to embrace nonviolence; by the sermon's conclusion, they have boldly taken that stand on their own.

Move One: False Prophets *Out There*

After reading his assigned text, Matthew 7:24-29, Taylor begins his sermon with what at first appears to be a prosaic and remarkably benign explication of the message centered on the familiar decision that it presents its readers: "Once we hear the words of Jesus, we can either choose to put them into practice, thus being like a wise builder who builds his house upon a rock, or we can choose not to put them into practice, thus being like a foolish builder who builds his house upon sand." That choice, of course, will be tested by the proverbial "harsh weather conditions" that reveal the "strength or weakness" of a life's foundation.

Building on the theme of the importance of words, within the structural motif of the "two ways," Taylor develops the major premise of the first part of his sermon, that there are two kinds of words, graceful words and angry words, the words of God and the words of Satan. The words of God bring peace and "move the world towards a healthy humanity." The words of Satan, "contaminated with evil intent," deceive and coerce, leading people to war. As "boxcars in the train of thought," Satan's words "carry toxic energy into the public square." In one subtle hint of what will come later in the sermon, Taylor states that these words lead "unsuspecting loyalists to support brutal activities that ruthlessly strike against the cheek of the Sermon on the Mount."

Taylor next narrows his explication of the two kinds of words by focusing on the agents through which Satan conveys his words to an unsuspecting public, described in traditional biblical language as "false prophets." Drawing upon the familiar story of the fall in Genesis 3, he observes that Satan "has upgraded his tactic from speaking his words through a single serpent to conveying his agenda through an entire den of serpents."

What is striking to this point is how non-threatening Taylor's sermon appears to be. He uses third person pronouns almost entirely as he exploits the familiar *topos* from which conservative Bible-believers have long drawn language to describe those with whom they disagree: The false prophets are *them*, and they are *out there*. In this way, Taylor and audience are insiders, joined together by their opposition to a common enemy.

Reinforcing this comfortable familiarity is Taylor's style of language and delivery. Although there are hints of the poetic language that we expect in the black sermon, the sentences are entirely declarative, with no direct exhortation whatsoever. To this point in the sermon, Taylor has not used a single personal pronoun. His claims are offered as impersonal, explanatory data—"just the facts." Likewise, the performative elements of the sermon lull the hearers into a state of complacency. His voice is low, his pace is slow and deliberate, and what tonal variations there are to this point are confined within a very narrow range. For a prophetic word, the sermon's vocal delivery to this point is remarkably gentle.

Toward the end of the first move, however, we get the first indication that the message is not so benign as the opening leads us to expect, as Taylor introduces the economic metaphor of the marketplace to explain the persistence of false prophets in the world: they continue their evil work in response to popular demand. This leads him to shift his focus from the false prophets to their customers: "religious consumers" who "tirelessly shop for doctrines of easy-isms." As he puts it, "They go from church to church like going from yard sale to yard sale, eagerly looking for smooth words that are for sale. They are shopping for words with smooth edges that will calmly caress their feelings of guilt that arise when they intentionally choose not to put into practice the words of Jesus."

To be sure, the offenders are still cast in the third person, yet Taylor's condemnation of their attempts to rationalize their failure to obey the clear instructions in the Sermon on the Mount begins to hit closer to home. Particularly telling is his charge that religious consumerism leads believers to reject the Sermon's clear call to nonviolence: "They bargain hunt for words that give them permission to seek the destruction not only of their actual persecutors, but also the destruction of anyone who could potentially propose a threat of persecuting them in the future."

Accentuating this feeling of transition are the vocal qualities of Taylor's delivery. His volume begins to rise and we begin to hear increased inflections of pitch and rhythm, infusing his message with the rising sense of urgency with which he utters the dire prediction that concludes the sermon's first move. Among the sins of these "religious consumers"—those who store up "treasures on earth in barns that grow bigger in each economic growth cycle" while watching with "apathetic indifference a bleeding and hungry Lazarus on their security cameras begging for mercy at the entrance to their beautifully adorned security gates"—is this singular transgression: "They shop for rainy words that water down the message of the Sermon on the Mount with such saturation that it causes moral mudslides in the lives of Christians, *leaving them unprepared to respond nonviolently in the presence of evil that exist[s] in our world today*" [emphasis added].

What we have in the sermon's first move, then, is a somewhat predictable and nonthreatening description of evil in the outside world, a description that no doubt would have been familiar to his audience and to which they would readily have given their full assent. Taylor occupies the role of their "tour guide," symbolically placing them in the position of standing alongside him and engaging in a shared condemnation of false teachers "out there." This merging of the positions of preacher and audience in a shared condemnation of the common enemy bolsters Taylor's own ethos, even as it prepares his hearers to experience shock at the possibility that they might be guilty of the same offenses.

Move Two: Apostasy *in Here*

Building upon the transition that concludes the sermon's first move, Taylor announces the theme of the sermon's second move and the essence of his prophetic indictment of middle-class American Christianity: Having exchanged their "kingdom consciousness for a cultural consciousness," American Christians have been "subliminally conditioned . . . to be willing to hate and to kill their enemies without mercy when it is deemed necessary." Having lost their radical commitment to living out the words of Jesus in the Sermon on the Mount, he fears, Christians "will have no way of storm-proofing our society against the social storms that are gathering on yonder horizon."

Taylor unfolds this theme by first observing that the presence of "violent and bloody clashes between warring factions in third world countries" should underscore the need for Christians to live out Jesus' message of nonviolence "within the context of our own nation." Indeed, as evidence that "our nation is possibly backsliding into the dangerous direction of social unrest," he points to airwaves "filled with ... the toxic words of anger" that threaten to turn "the American melting pot into the American boiling pot." He then rebukes the preachers of his own tradition—many of whom are sitting in his audience—for their failure to confront these pressing social problems: "While these pulpits of the airwaves are sounding their message with great volume, many of our pulpits in the churches have become shamefully timid and strangely silent in proclaiming the gospel of peace and reconciliation in regards to race, gender, politics, and religion." Although his indictment is framed somewhat abstractly as "our pulpits," his point is clear: Instead of challenging the dominant culture, Christian leaders have timidly acquiesced to its militaristic ideology. This leads him to issue what is not only the climactic pronouncement of move two but the "thesis" of the entire sermon, which takes the form of a dramatic plea for preachers to fulfill their calling as agents of social change: "Preachers must not be afraid to loudly proclaim from the rooftops that the church of Jesus Christ is built upon the solid foundation of a nonviolent Christ, who is the Prince of Peace."

Move two thus shifts the focus of the sermon to the failure of the members of his own religious tradition—indeed, the members of his own audience—to stand against the descent of their society into a culture of violence. At this point, the sermon becomes dramatically personal, as we face the possibility that what we thought was *"out there"* is actually happening *"in here."* Two elements in Taylor's style of language and delivery accentuate this shift.

First is his sudden and pervasive use of personal pronouns. Whereas move one contained almost no personal references, move two is filled with them. "*I* am afraid," he tells his audience. He warns of the coming storms that will threaten "the foundations of *our* well-constructed lives." Reports of violence in the developing world should convince *us* of the need to live out the teachings of Jesus in the context of *our* nation. At several points, Taylor subtly links and interweaves references to his own audience—"us"—with the Christian consumers—"them"—who were the focus of the indictment issued in move one: "Unless Christians [them] remain radically committed to living the Sermon on the Mount in this nation, *we* will have no way of storm-proofing *our* society against the social storms that are gathering on yonder horizon." He similarly interweaves the third and first person when he addresses the failure of preachers to confront the culture's descent into violence: "Preachers must not be afraid to . . . proclaim . . . that the Church of Jesus Christ is built upon the solid foundation of a nonviolent Christ," he insists, for "*our* nation and *our* world cannot afford to go long without hearing the words of Jesus preached. How shall they hear these words without a preacher, and how shall *we* preach the words of Jesus with love unless *we* encounter the God of peace and become intuitively one with his feelings and with his passions for a wounded and fragmented humanity?" [Emphasis added here and above.] Thus, whereas in move one, Taylor and his audience stand together in a critique of the outside world's false teachers and the "Christian consumers" whose demand for comforting reassurance keeps those false teachers in business, in move two Taylor turns the critique on the members of his own audience who now share in the guilt of the outside world.

Taylor also underscores this shift with the vocal elements of his delivery, which continue to infuse the message with tension and urgency. In contrast to his more monotonic delivery at the beginning of the sermon, Taylor's voice in move two rises and falls with noticeable variations in volume and pitch. He pounds particular words and accents important phrases with strategic pauses that highlight their significance. When, for example, he proclaims that Christians must live out the Sermon on the Mount "within the context of our own nation"—he shouts the word "own" in a way that imbues that call with particular urgency. In a line (represented graphically to illustrate his use of accent), Taylor calls out to the audience for support as he insists that preachers must not be intimidated by the "livid media personalities" who have such influence

> over the **P**eople / who **S**it / in the **P**ews / from Sunday to Sunday (help me somebody!).

In his climactic call for preachers to proclaim loudly that the church is built on the "solid foundation of a nonviolent Christ, who is the Prince of Peace," he elongates the word "is," almost transforming it into a diphthong that is more sung than spoken—to which his audience responds with applause. When he raises the sobering question, which concludes move two, of what will happen if preachers fail to preach the words of Jesus to their society, he at first shouts that question, each word again punctuated by pauses that are pregnant with tension, but then quiets his voice to almost a whisper, all in a way that accentuates the gravity of his plea:

> **H**ow / **S**hall / **T**hey / **H**ear these words without a preacher?

Whereas in move one, Taylor offers an almost emotionless recounting of the "facts," here we encounter the passionate voice of the prophet, alternatively thundering with indignation at the sins of God's people and earnestly pleading with them to return to the mission to which God has called them.

In this way, Taylor in move two transforms the audience's symbolic position from standing with him and passing judgment on the outside world to being identified with those very false prophets whom they have just condemned. Taylor now stands above or, at least, at a distance from his audience, as he passionately confronts them with this painful reality: Like the consumerist Christians in move one who have bought words that rationalize away the clear teachings of Jesus, his own hearers are in danger of backsliding into the same culture of violence for which the world now stands under judgment. At the same time, however, Taylor is careful in the way that he frames this confrontation. Deftly avoiding danger, inherent in his rhetorical situation, that he will alienate his audience, he rejects a frontal assault on his hearers. At no point does he employ the second person pronoun, "you," to assail them directly. Instead, his warnings are couched as expressions of personal concern: "I am afraid." Although in one sense he stands apart from them with the objectivity of distance needed to diagnose their condition, in another sense he includes himself in his indictment by using first person plural pronouns to issue his warnings, which are themselves largely hypothetical: "*We* will have no way of storm-proofing our society." Using abstract language, he refers to Christian leaders as "our pulpits"; rather than saying "*you* must not be afraid," he insists that "*preachers* must not be afraid" to call Christians to nonviolence (emphasis added, here and above). Taylor thus seeks to warn his audience in the strongest terms possible without attacking them directly, leaving the door open for the transformation that he will create in the sermon's third move, a transformation that will symbolically bring his hearers back to his side, chastened and prepared to proclaim with one voice their determination to stand for truth of the gospel.

Move Three: *We* will stand with Jesus.

In move three, Taylor answers the question that ends the sermon's second move— "How shall they hear these words without a preacher?"—with this bold proclamation: "As preachers of the nonviolent Christ, we will lift up our voices even if we have to sing a solo of a new song in the face of an angry chorus of voices that insist on singing the same old tired song of racial, religious, and political division." In a poignant turn of phrase, he expresses collective repentance on the part of Christian leaders who have failed in their prophetic calling, recasting their silence as itself an act of violence: "As preachers of the words of Jesus, we will no longer practice the violence of silence while watching hate-mongers spread their venomous malice all over this land." He expresses communal resolve on behalf of the church to advocate for the oppressed, "God's offspring in this country and around the world," to confront the wealthy who "seek to ride the 'serf' board of greed upon the massive wave of global wealth that is being pushed inland by the high tide of cheap labor," and to challenge Christians to withdraw their "allegiance from institutions that demand the surrender of soul and integrity for the preservation of any kingdom that is of this world." Most of all, he gives voice to a new determination on the part of the church, trusting not in Constantine but in Christ as the "protector and defender of his followers," to risk actually putting into practice the Sermon on the Mount's call to nonviolence, "come hail or high water."

As with his earlier moves, Taylor signals the shift to move three stylistically through his lexical choices and mode of delivery. He initially expresses collective determination in a cascade of resolutions all couched in the second person plural active voice:

> We will lift our voices ... We will no longer practice the violence of silence ... We will speak words of truth ... We will peacefully confront ... We will encourage all Christians ... We will not fight for the right to bear arms, but we will fight for the right of all races and political persuasions to lock arms in peace ... We will arm ourselves with the nonviolent weapons, which we will call the sword of the Spirit, which is the word of God, and is able to pull down strongholds.

From this point on, Taylor's language is entirely framed as a proclamation of what "we" resolve to do.

Even more pronounced than his lexical choices are the vocal inflections with which Taylor brings the sermon to its emotionally charged conclusion. Indeed, we find in his conclusion a hint of that feature of black preaching that W. E. B. Du Bois called "the Frenzy" when, as Lischer put it, "the *experience* of God replaces *talk about* God."[4] Taylor slides into black dialect as he challenges God's people to sing a "new song in the face of an angry chorus of voices that insist on singin' the same tired song of racial, religious, and political division" and when, in his final sentence, he exclaims, "Now we goin' stand right here until he comes to take us home with him." At several points, he injects dialogic exclamations, familiar in black preaching, to engage his audience: "The same God who protected and defended Shadrach, Meshach, and Abednego in the fiery furnace is still able to protect us in this age of terrorism! *(Help me somebody!)*" (emphasis added). His volume continues to rise and he powerfully accentuates key words so that at times he is shouting, as when he reminds his hearers, "Jesus said, 'On this rock **I** / **Will** / **Build** / **My** / **Church**, and the gates of hell shall not prevail against it.' The church does not need to be afraid of hell. Hell ought to be afraid of the Church!"—a pronouncement that elicits thunderous, sustained applause from his audience. All of this culminates in a final declaration of communal resolve, more sung than spoken, built around the repetition of the phrase, "We will stand":

> We will stand on the solid rock. We will stand on the solid rock when mean-spirited words form a severe emotional weather system that moves across this country and world, endangering all expression of spiritual life. We will stand on the rock. We will stand on the solid rock when hateful words from our enemies fall around us like raindrops from a pregnant storm cloud. We will stand on the solid rock. We will stand on the solid rock when the meteor-sized hail of bitter oppression leaves huge dents in our desire to forgive those who have trespassed against us. We will by the power of God's Holy Spirit stand on the rock. We will stand on the rock when the waters of persecutions are

> rising and Katrina-like winds of rage are blowing against us.
> We will stand on the rock.

With this climactic proclamation, it is as if the hearers themselves shout their determination to embrace with courage the life of nonviolence.

Particularly striking is the militant tone that pervades this final expression of *parrhesia*. The language is active, filled with verbs like sing, speak, confront, and, especially, stand. Even quiescent acceptance of the culture's norms is transformed into a "practice" of the "violence of silence." Taylor's conclusion is laced with the language of war: "we will fight for the right of all races and political persuasions to lock arms in peace"; "we will arm ourselves with . . . nonviolent weapons"; we will take up the "sword of the Spirit" which is able to "pull down strongholds"; we will trust that "Christ is the protector and defender of his followers." Taylor envisions a church so boldly empowered that it strikes fear into the heart of hell itself: "The church does not need to be afraid of hell. Hell ought to be afraid of the church." In this way, Taylor reframes nonviolence so that, instead of reflecting weakness and passivity, it becomes a demonstration of strength and defiance, captured in the promise that the church will "peacefully confront" those whose greed brings suffering and violence to the world.

Move three, then, effects the final transformation of the audience's relationship to the preacher and to the world, expressed in the church's defiant proclamation that it will stand against evil in its culture. Taylor creates this symbolic, communal expression of resolve by using the classic trope, *prosopopeia*, a rhetorical device through which a rhetor addresses an imaginary audience for the sake of his or her actual audience. In this case, Taylor speaks to the world "out there." But he does so in a way that brings the audience back to the position that it occupied in the speech's first move, standing alongside him and facing that world. Except this time, the audience's role has changed. Instead of being passive observers to his condemnation of false teachers and religious consumers, now the audience symbolically occupies the podium with him, proclaiming through his voice their impassioned commitment to put the words of Jesus into practice.

Conclusion

When Jerry Taylor stood before his audience that evening, he confronted the two crucial questions that ought to be at the heart of every preacher's sermon preparation: First, how can I gain a hearing for my text? Second, how can I enable my audience not only to understand the text, but much more, to *experience* it? In other words, how do I use language, voice, and body to craft a sermon such that, in the moment of its hearing, the audience experiences the truth of the text not just intellectually, but also emotionally?

For Taylor, the first question was particularly daunting: How does one bring an unwelcome message to a potentially resistant audience? Taylor's text could have been heard as nothing more than unsettling and offensive—a sermon intended to inflict the comfortable and not comfort the afflicted since his hearers had come expecting pastoral comfort and not a prophetic rebuke. Given Taylor's rhetorical situation, the audience might easily have rejected both message and messenger. Although he might have taken the route of a John the Baptist—"You brood of vipers!" (Matt. 3:7)—he instead crafted a sermon that followed a different biblical model, that of Amos who, for the benefit of his Israelite audience, first condemned Israel's neighbors ("For three sins of Damascus ... Gaza ... Tyre ... Edom," and the like, "I will not turn back [my wrath]"), and then in words that would have been particularly delicious to his hearers, denounced Israel's special enemy, Judah, before turning his attention to his real audience, Israel herself (see Amos 1-2). It was also the strategy of Paul in Romans 1-3, who shouts condemnation on the Gentiles, drawing upon a familiar litany of pagan sins, before probing the sin of his true target, "you ... [who] call yourself a Jew" (Rom. 2:17). In both cases, the biblical writers bring their hearers alongside them in condemnation of a common enemy and only then do they turn their focus on the true audience they hope to reach. Taylor likewise first presents his hearers with a familiar and nonthreatening pronouncement of judgment on false teachers out in the world and on the consumerist Christians whose demand for easy words keeps those false teachers in business. Only when his hearers symbolically stand with him does he raise the possibility that they have been guilty of the same practices, which is the focus of the sermon's second move. By raising that possibility, of course, Taylor hopes to provoke dissonance and discomfort in his audience when they see the incongruity between their supposed status as insiders to the kingdom of God and their actual behavior, which identifies them more with the outsiders whose practices they have just condemned. Of course, this discomfort can be resolved in a renewed expression of commitment to take the words of Jesus seriously, which Taylor develops in the sermon's third move.

The second question, how to help his audience experience rather than merely learn *about* the text, Taylor answers by constructing a discourse that symbolically places them in a position of defiantly expressing that commitment themselves, a process that reaches its climactic point at the sermon's conclusion. There, Taylor draws upon the resources of the African American preaching tradition to create what Henry Mitchell called the "one aspect of the sermon that most nearly deserves to be called typically Black"—the celebration, through which the preacher ensures that the sermon's ideas have been "etched by ecstasy on the heart of the hearer."[5] Taylor crafts a conclusion that gives his audience an emotion filled glimpse of the courage that will be needed to stand against overwhelming currents in contemporary U.S. culture. In the sermon's final moment, it is not as if the audience is hearing Taylor urge them to take a stand; rather, in his voice, they symbolically shout their own resolve. What is more, Taylor co-opts the militarist language and tone of the dominant culture and uses it to express his call to bold nonviolence, a strategy that potentially allows his hearers to actually *feel* that courage. In this final transcendent moment, abstract theological ideas become real in the audience's experience. Rather than accepting or even retreating from the violence in their culture, Christians, fiercely committed to peace, shake their fist at the forces of evil in the world and say, "Bring 'em on."

2

The Song of the Vineyard

Compositional Notes

This sermon was preached at the North Davis Church of Christ in Arlington, Texas, on January 17, 2010. The North Davis Church is a predominantly white congregation. I was asked to serve as the principal speaker for the Hubert Moss Ecumenical Service. This is a gathering of Arlington ministers to celebrate the legacy of Dr. Martin Luther King Jr.

Communication with Walter Brueggemann about this text helped me see the total significance of the parabolic nature of Isaiah 5:1-7. The explicit imagery richly embedded throughout the full length of the text provides an expansive vocabulary from which I extracted language that moves the message from a generic parabolic idea to a concretized prophetic point.

Isaiah empathetically stands in Yahweh's shoes and creatively expresses what he perceives as a divine reaction to the disappointing fruitlessness of Israel's social righteousness. Isaiah's metaphor of a musical rendition portrays his prophetic performance as an act of "lip singing" for Yahweh. Yahweh provides the lyrical utterances as the prophet surrenders the instrumentation of his mouth that moves in rhythmic syncopation with the divine lover's passionate yearning for his beloved Israel to give birth to the offspring of social justice.

The broken-hearted singer sings a sad song that sounds a lot like a genre of African American music known as the Blues. The song is filled with lyrics that express both disappointment and retribution. Israel is going to be abandoned by God for its failure to bring forth the good grapes of a healthy life-affirming community. It is at this critical juncture of the text that Brueggemann prompted me to faithfully proceed with the daunting task of prophetic preaching by summoning the courage to make application.

Nevertheless, Isaiah's severe words of condemnation presented a unique challenge. How would I communicate the word of judgment clearly evident in the textual content of the sermon? If America is found to be as guilty as Israel is in the text should I present the same prophetic conclusion about America that Isaiah did concerning Israel? Is there a way to be excused from making the pronouncement of judgment? Is there an escape clause in the text, that provides the opportunity for me to end the sermon with "God Bless America"?

THE SONG OF THE VINEYARD

Isaiah 5:1-7

In Isaiah 5:1 the prophet describes himself as a singer. The prophet's song can be classified as "prophetic blues." Isaiah writes with pain-scarred lyrics a sad song that dramatizes the strained relationship between God and his beloved. The song is filled with penetrating words of truth that poetically describe God's broken heart. God's heart is broken by the fruitless failure of Israel to produce the fruit of justice, love, mercy, and righteousness.

Isaiah's melancholic tune makes it clear that, even though Israel is God's chosen people, Israel fails to consistently live up to God's expectations. Israel as a nation fails to understand that it was not planted as a vineyard for its own nationalistic self consumption. Yahweh intends Israel as a vineyard to produce the non-toxic drink of genuine human community.

Other nations of the earth are to consume this grand example of national compassion and healthy human interactions. When all the nations of the earth are filled with the qualitative substance of Israel's national example they too will bow their governmental knees to God's will. When this happens we will see the mighty in-breaking of the reign and rule of God on earth as it is in heaven. We will see human community resting upon the solid foundation of the enduring principles of love, mercy, justice, and righteousness.

In light of our text, we will first observe how the prophet's song painstakingly recalls the careful agricultural steps the owner of the vineyard takes to cultivate the best outcome for the vineyard's productivity. Next, we will pay attention to the ways in which Israel as the vineyard fails to satisfy Yahweh's hopeful expectations for being the nation that would model for the world an example of true human community. Finally, we will observe the painful and disastrous consequences of Israel's failure to produce the national and global fruit of justice and righteousness.

Isaiah's opening pitch directs our attention to the agricultural quality of the vineyard's location. The vineyard is not planted in a barren desert. It is planted in the best agricultural environment possible. The vineyard is planted on a "fertile hillside."

Putting things in environments where they are most likely to grow is consistent with God's nature as creator. In the Genesis account of creation God plants the first human couple in Eden.

Eden was replete with healthy produce perfect for human consumption. The rich vegetation in Eden had not been contaminated by the toxic chemicals and pesticides produced by corporations who care more about making money than they care about making foods that are safe for human consumption!

God has planted his church on a fertile hillside in America. There are gigantic church steeples sprouting up all over this nation that bear testimony to the wealth and prosperity of American Christians.

Like his expectation of the vineyard, God expects the church in America to produce healthy fruit for spiritual consumption. The world is thirsty for a model of human community permeated with justice and righteousness.

The second verse of Isaiah's song says that "The owner dug up the fertile hillside and cleared it of stones and planted it with the choicest vines." The ground is broken up. The soil is softened and cleared of stones. Every hard stone that could obstruct the vineyard from properly receiving Yahweh's rich investment of choicest vines is removed.

As we gaze upon the recent landscape of American history, we see the removal of many rocks and stones that obstructed this country from becoming a nation of public compassion, justice, and righteousness.

- Historic legislation cleared away the oppressive stone of child labor practices in America that once exploited children for economic profit.
- Historic legislation cleared away the heavy stone of legalized gender discrimination in America that once treated women as second-class citizens.
- Landmark legislation cleared away the giant rock of racial discrimination in America that once allowed African Americans to be treated worse than tamed animals.
- Compassionate legislation cleared away the stone of elderly neglect in America that once allowed our senior citizens to suffer from inadequate health care.
- Courageous legislation cleared away the boulder of racial slavery in America that made it possible for a dignified relationship to exist between sons and daughters of former slaves and former slave owners.

What will our national religious and political leaders do with the American landscape now that it has been prepared for a greater productivity of public compassion? The church as God's vineyard in America is perfectly positioned to inspire this nation to new levels of justice and righteousness.

Next Isaiah says that once Yahweh plants the hillside with the choicest vines he establishes a watchtower for protection and surveillance. Yahweh intends to protect his most precious investment against religious and political vandalism. We notice God's protective care of Israel as a vineyard when Isaiah says, "the Lord enters into judgment against the elders and leaders of his people: It is you who have ruined my vineyard; the plunder from the poor is in your houses. What do you mean by crushing my people and grinding the faces of the poor?" (3:14).

Yahweh sees from his watchtower how the religious and political leaders practice injustice and bloodshed which leads to the moral decline of Israel.

God sees Israel's leaders filled with selfish ambition invading the vineyard like a swarming pestilence immune to every possible repellent. The leaders of Israel took plunder from the poor and stashed it away in their luxurious palaces. They crushed God's people and scrubbed the faces of the poor into the ground.

What does God see when he observes America from his watchtower? What kind of behavior does God see when he looks upon the conduct of the religious, political, and corporate leaders in America?

- How much of the plunder from the poor is stashed away in the houses of religious leaders?
- How much of the plunder from the poor is used to enrich the luxurious lifestyles of corrupt politicians and their co-conspirators?
- How much of the plunder from the poor is used to secure fabulous homes for Wall Street barons while the poor remain homeless, hungry, sick, and unemployed?
- How much of the plunder from the massive bailouts is stashed away in the stock options of the banking industry tycoons?
- How much plunder has been taken from unsuspecting homebuyers through the adjustable mortgage scandal and conveniently hidden in the deep pockets of those who constructed one of the biggest global financial scams in world history?
- How much plunder has been taken from poor customers at the gas pumps by oil chieftains and their companies who are making record profits in the billions even during an economic recession?

- How much plunder has been taken from "illegal immigrants" by those who like ticks grow fat from sucking the blood from the back of cheap labor?

After Isaiah sings about the building of a watchtower, he sings a powerful stanza that expresses Yahweh's great expectant hope in Israel's potential. Yahweh anticipates that Israel will quench the thirst in the world by producing the sweet drink of national compassion, justice, mercy, and righteousness.

Just as expectant parents prepare their child's room before it is born, God shows confident hope by cutting out a winepress in the vineyard. He makes preparation to receive the fruit of his labor.

What is God's expectant hope for the church that he has planted in America? When he looks upon the church in America does he see the fulfillment of his original design or does he see a squandered investment gone bad? Does he see a productive vineyard that is producing the joyful fruit of unity, harmony, love, brother and sisterhood from sea to shining sea or does God see Christians divided against one other: red states and blue states?

Are we producing the sweet drink of reconciliation or are we bringing forth the sour juice of racial hostility and political division?

The singing prophet comes to the climax of his song which describes Yahweh's painful disappointment in the vineyard. The lyrics of the song go like this: "He looked for a crop of good grapes, but it yielded only bad fruit." Israel's voluptuous potential as a nation of compassion had shrunk into a wrinkled raisin of injustice. Israel as the vineyard produced the shriveled fruit of economic exploitation. It also produced the bitter drink of national neglect of the fatherless and the widow.

In the twisted face of this devastating disappointment Isaiah moves to the third verse in his song to describe Yahweh's reaction. God says, "Now you dwellers in Jerusalem and men of Judah, judge between me and my vineyard. What more could have been done for my vineyard than I have done for it?"

Yahweh is like a good parent who wants to understand why his child displays unproductive behavior despite all he has done to raise Israel correctly. God as a good parent raised Israel in a healthy environment with all the support needed for growth and development as a nation.

God properly concludes that he provided Israel as his vineyard with everything necessary to bring about the good grapes of human compassion. Yahweh correctly believes that the vineyard has no excuse for its failure to produce healthy grapes.

Isaiah has to clear his throat before he sings the harsh lyrics of condemnation in verses 5 and 6. The prophet's voice does not crack at all as it bellows out the consequences the vineyard must face as a result of its failure to produce good grapes.

The singing prophet knows that once he finishes his rendition his audience will not give him a standing ovation. He already knows that his message is going to be met with resistance. They will pick up the stones cleared from the hillside and hurl them at him for speaking the bold truth during a time when truth is not desired.

God says "I will tell you what I am going to do to my vineyard: I will take away its hedge, and it will be destroyed; I will break down its wall, and it will be trampled. I will make it a wasteland, neither pruned nor cultivated, and briers and thorns will grow there. I will command the clouds not to rain on it."

These are harsh and frightening words for Israel to hear. God says he is going to take his hands off of the nation that refuses to comply with his vision of justice and righteousness. He says he will break down its wall and allow it to be trampled. God will not let his rain fall upon it. We can only imagine the sense of fear and desperation Israel must have felt when hearing these words.

Isaiah explains the meaning of his song in verse 7. He says, "The vineyard of the Lord Almighty is the house of Israel, and the men of

Judah are the garden of his delight. And he looked for justice, but saw bloodshed; for righteousness, but heard cries of distress."

The church within every nation is the garden of his delight.

- When God looks at the land in which Christians live, does he see righteousness or does he hear the cries of distress coming from those being exploited?
- Does God see mercy in our land for those losing their homes and jobs or does he see apathy and indifference towards those genuinely in need of our compassion?
- Does God see generosity in our land for the devastated Haitians, who before the massive earthquake were dying by the thousands in the towering shadow of our affluence and prosperity?
- When God looks at the land in which Christians live, does he see justice or does he see bloodshed?
- Does God see justice or bloodshed when he sees people in our nation who pay their insurance premiums in full and on time only for insurance companies to tell them they have a disease or need a life-saving surgery not covered by their policy?

When in Cape Town South Africa I observed people living in abject poverty and crime in the enormous townships on the outskirts of the city. I was shaken to the core when told that Cape Town had recently completed the construction of a $600 million dollar stadium to host the 2010 FIFA World Cup.

This is similar to the recent construction of the new Texas Stadium in Arlington, Texas. Originally estimated to cost $650 *million* dollars, the stadium's current construction cost was $1.15 *billion* dollars, making it one of the most expensive sports venues ever built.

We should ask, what does God see when he looks at these situations?

- Does he see justice or bloodshed when billions of dollars are spent on sports facilities while there are untold millions living without the basic necessities for human survival?
- Does he see justice or bloodshed when we spend more money on facilities built for entertainment than we spend on putting food in the bloated stomachs of starving children in the Appalachians, the Mississippi Delta, South Africa, or south Dallas?

Let the church in every nation be the vineyard that will produce the fruit of justice, righteousness, and mercy.

- Let the church in every nation be that city that sits on a hill.
- Let the church in America join in singing the prophet's song of a productive vineyard.
- Let the church in America sing the song of justice and mercy so loudly that it will shake the foundations on Capitol Hill in Washington D.C.
- Let the church in every state sing the song of justice and mercy so loudly that it will be heard in the legislative halls in every state capitol.
- Let the church go beyond singing the song of justice and mercy to the choir.
- Let us take this beautiful melody beyond our buildings into the streets and sing it at the top of our voices.
- Let us sing the song of justice and righteousness on our jobs, in our homes, at school, at city hall, in the board room, and everywhere we may go.

This is a prerequisite for God to favorably respond to the request, "God bless America." Isaiah reminds us that in order for God to bless

America as a nation we must produce the national fruit of justice for all, righteousness for all, mercy for all, and compassion for all regardless of their gender, race, religion, politics, class, citizenship, or sexual orientation.

Isaiah's message is that if we as Yahweh's vineyard fail to produce the healing fruit of public compassion he will hang a sign on the entrance of the vineyard that reads, "No Trespassing. This is Condemned Property Due to Lack of Compassionate Productivity!"

"THE SONG OF THE VINEYARD"

A Critical Biblical Response

Walter Brueggemann

Jerry Taylor has written a challenging, summoning sermon on the famous passage, "The Song of the Vineyard."

I.

It is clear that Taylor has focused on the primary accent points of the text and has exposited them in a compelling, persuasive way:

1. God, in *God's generosity*, has taken the initiative and through careful preparations has created a fecund context in which Israel may live a productive, obedient life.

2. *Israel has failed* to produce what God had expected, because Israel has been resistant to God's intention for Israel's life.

3. *God is deeply disappointed* and so the relationship with Israel is placed in acute jeopardy.

With these accent points, Taylor has walked through the text with attentiveness, in a way that the "message" of the text is ready at hand for an alert listener.

II.

I came to the sermon hoping the preacher would linger long over the particularity of the text and that the sermon would not remain too much at a generic level. I was not disappointed.

1. It is worth noticing that the text is parabolic in two senses. First, it is parabolic about a vineyard and the owner of the vineyard. The imagery more fully suggests that the vineyard in fact has no life of its own, but exists only by the goodness of the owner and for the purposes

of the owner. For reasons we are not told, the vineyard refused its true character in response to the owner. Second, at a parabolic level, the text is a "love song" whereby the owner serenades and woos the vineyard. We may imagine the owner strumming a song. For that reason we may also imagine that God is a wounded, deeply disappointed lover. Even though the owner decided the vineyard must be terminated and rooted up, there is a sense of loss for the owner, otherwise he would not have sung a love song in the first place.

2. The pay-off of the parable is the twice-repeated "wild grapes" (vv. 2, 4). Taylor lingers over the imagery of fruit that is shriveled and dry and sour with powerful and evocative language when he says, "Israel's voluptuous potential as a nation of compassion had shrunk into a wrinkled raisin of injustice." No wonder the owner is chagrined and wounded and the preacher has captured this with visual splendor.

3. The love song ends in a word play. That word play cannot be reproduced in English, but it is nonetheless instructive. The word pair in verse 7, "justice-bloodshed," is in Hebrew *mispat-mispah;* the second word pair, "righteousness-cry" is in Hebrew *sedeqah-za'aqah.* In both cases, the poet has found words that sound nearly alike. The reason the two word pairs are important is that they tell the nature of the "wild grapes." The bad produce is quite specific; it is *a society of violence* (bloodshed, cry) in which the vulnerable and helpless are mistreated, perhaps by direct street violence, more likely by exploitative labor practices and bad economic policies. The bad produce is a distorted, anti-human society. By contrast, what the owner wanted is "justice and righteousness," *policies and practices of neighborliness* that protect the poor and give dignity to the weak. This is congruent with the rest of the prophetic message. Thus the word play adds "bite" to the poetry which Taylor unpacks with his own litany of penetrating questions, "Does God see mercy in our land for those losing their homes and jobs or does he see apathy and indifference towards those genuinely in need of our compassion." Like us, Israel was faced with the stark choice of violence or neighborliness.

III.

The parable ends with radical and harsh judgment: the vineyard is abandoned and destroyed. In context this refers to the destruction of Jerusalem and the regime of David. The word is that Israel (and then the church; and then the United States) will be abandoned by God for its refusal to produce the good grapes of neighborliness.

This is a very hard word. But the preacher deepens his inquiry into the abandonment of the vineyard with an unstated acknowledgment of Isaiah 27:2-4 where the prophet reuses the theme of the vineyard. In that usage God comes back to the abandoned vineyard and vows to be its keeper and guard. All that is required in this usage is that the vineyard must "make peace with me." The formula is stated twice. The preacher introduces his reflections on what has to happen to make peace with God with his promising phrase, "There is prerequisite for God to favorably respond to the request, 'God bless America.'" The prophets, here and elsewhere, contend that peace with God depends upon justice and righteousness for the neighbor. We love God by loving neighbor. By the time of the second use of the theme in chapter 27, Israel may be in a position to do what it had refused at the beginning, namely, to care for the neighborhood in public ways. That is the "good grapes" for which the owner waits and watches.

3

What Does the Lord Require?

Compositional Notes

This message was delivered on September 16, 2007, at the Abilene Christian University Lectureship in Abilene, Texas: the first time in the one-hundred-year history of the program that an African American served as the opening night theme speaker.

Micah 6:1-8 provides the opportunity to address religious hypocrisy and economic injustice. My urgent desire to speak to these issues takes me directly into the text at the outset of the sermon. It is important for me to quickly establish in the audience's mind a connection with the idea that Israel has wronged Yahweh. It is also important for the listener to see immediately that the nation is being tried in the cosmic courtroom of justice in 6:1-2. A high mountain of evidence is stacked against the defendant. The facts prove beyond circumstantial evidence that Israel's faulty religion allows her to commit crimes against the most vulnerable within the Hebrew society.

In Micah 6:3-4 the prophet raises a critical question, "What have I done to you that make you act unjustly? How have I burdened you?" These verses are emphasized at this stage in the sermon because I want to point the thinking of the audience toward the prophet's closing question in 6:7, "What does the Lord require?" I see the opening and closing questions serving as two bookends with textual content sandwiched between, all providing a vibrant biblical critique of Israel's religion *and* the American brand of Christianity.

In Micah 6:5 the prophet's call for Israel to "remember the journey" alludes to the charge that Yahweh's worshipers allow injustices to exist because they fail to remember God's liberating acts during the Exodus. As the national memory of God's liberation decreases, a nation loses concern for justice, love, and mercy. I seek to make the case that American injustice is a credible sign of memory loss of the mighty blessings that God has bountifully showered on this nation.

In 2007 the American practice of political corruption and economic exploitation in the form of religious and corporate greed had reached dangerous heights. American monetary greed was openly uncovered and seen in the ugly forms of insider trading, subprime lending, and predatory lending. American conservative evangelical religion was passively silent in the face of this national moral crisis. Evangelical Christianity looked like an identical twin to the religion of Micah's day. This understanding motivated me to raise the question, What does the Lord require of the American church today? Does our emotional worship assembly cause God to close his eyes to the unregulated greed and injustice that many American Christians have learned to wink at? Does God enjoy million-dollar church buildings and entertaining worship or does he desire love, justice, and mercy?

WHAT DOES THE LORD REQUIRE?

Micah 6:1-8

According to Micah the temple of Israel has lost its moral authority. It has been co-opted by immoral men motivated by unspiritual aspirations. Despite the temple's spiritual corruption, Israel holds on to the empty forms of a morally bankrupt religion. In fact, Israel appears to be so religious that it could easily include in its pledge of allegiance the phrase, "One nation, under Yahweh, indivisible, with Liberty and Justice for All."

However, Micah reveals that Israel's theocratic society fails to practice liberty and justice *for all*. Israel's justice system only provides justice for the rich and powerful. Israel dresses its distorted justice in the long, black robe of economic exploitation. The Jewish merchants in Micah engage in price gouging. Corrupt trading practices are driven by unregulated greed. Merchants cheat their customers by using false weights and rigged measurements. A similar practice is carried on by some American companies. Consumers are paying more at the pump and getting less in the tank.

In Micah 6:1-8 the prophet boldly claims that the temple, the cultic center of Israel, has failed to stave off domestic injustice. Social injustice is rushing in upon the poor and powerless in Israel like the rising flood waters of Hurricane Katrina. Poor Jews with no resources to defend themselves are being driven out of their homes and off their lands. They are being cut down and uprooted like precious timber in the name of economic development and material progress.

As we study Micah's message, let us ask how the church in America is similar to the temple in Israel. Has the church in America lost its prophetic voice? In its pursuit of wealth and prosperity has the church in America become deaf, mute, and blind to the injustices perpetrated against the poor and powerless? Does the church remain silent in the face of Native Americans who are locked in abject poverty on "Indian Reservations" scattered across the United States? Despite the American church's aggressive missionary zeal, does it ignore situations of injustice practiced by American corporations that infiltrate African nations, essentially taking the natural resources from under their feet?

In many instances the church in America lends passive consent to the institutional powers and political interests that crush the poor underneath the heels of economic greed. We hope that Micah will provoke the church to rediscover its prophetic office. The church must no longer permit political pimps to turn the temple of the living God into a whore who sells herself to the highest bidder.

In Micah 6:1-2, the prophet describes the context of the cosmic courtroom where Yahweh makes his case against Israel. Like a prosecuting attorney pressing a guilty defendant, God questions Israel before nature's jury consisting of the mountains, the hills, and the foundations of the earth. It is proved beyond circumstantial evidence that Israel has committed crimes against nature—God's compassionate nature—by failing to show compassion upon the most vulnerable in her midst.

God says, "What have I done to you that make you act unjustly?" "How have I burdened you?" (Micah 6:3-4). Did I do too much for you when I delivered you from Egyptian oppression? Did I disrupt your false comfort in Egypt when I called you out to enter a fresh land that flows with milk and honey? Have I spoiled you as my only child by lavishing you with too much affection? Have the luxuries I have given to you made you lazy in the work of justice?

I imagine God asking the church in America a similar set of questions.

- Did the outpouring of my bountiful blessings upon you cause you to become insensitive to the needs of the alien stranger in your midst?

- Have you become so prideful in living in the greatest nation on earth that you view international humility as a political liability?
- Has your connection with superpower status made you so arrogant that you cannot walk humbly before your God?
- Did I grant you domestic peace for you to be concerned about advancing democracy only in the third-world countries that will allow American businesses and corporations to benefit from their natural resources?
- What have I done to you for you to act so unjustly?

Micah explains the basic cause of Israel's social injustice (6:5). He says that Israel is suffering from memory loss. Micah takes Israel back to the Exodus event where God shows mercy on Israel and delivers her from the despotic system of Egyptian oppression. Micah helps Israel to remember the non-oppressive leadership God appointed to the ancient Hebrews in the persons of Moses, Aaron, and Miriam. Micah wants Israel to see how the Mosaic legacy of humility, love, and justice is being disgraced by domestic oppression of God's people by their own leaders.

Israel is advised to "remember the journey."

- "Remember the journey." Remember how God delivered your ancestors from oppression and injustice on the other side of the Red Sea.
- "Remember the journey." Remember how Balak king of Moab counseled Balaam to curse Israel, but I would not let him.
- "Remember the journey." Remember how I protected you in the wilderness from starvation and dehydration.
- "Remember the journey." Remember how I gave you liberty instead of death when the British were coming.
- "Remember the journey." Remember how I cut the disease of slavery out of your body politic and made you one nation.

- "Remember the journey." Remember how I tore down the walls of segregation that contained graffiti written by the unjust hand of historical hatred.
- "Remember the journey." Remember how I kept you through two world wars, a great depression, the Cuban missile crisis, 9/11, and the global economic meltdown of 2008!

In Micah 6:6-7 the prophet describes Israel's religious value system. He gives us an inside view of the religious mindset that believes it can both worship God and practice injustice against the neighbor simultaneously. Israel is secure in the assumption that Yahweh's wrath against injustice can be appeased by what they give to him in their religious ceremonies.

Israel asks the question: "With what shall I come before the LORD and bow down before the exalted God? Shall I come before him with burnt offerings, with calves a year old? Will the LORD be pleased with thousands of rams, with ten thousand rivers of oil? Shall I offer my first born for my transgression, the fruit of my body for the sin of my soul?"

Israel's list of things that can be offered as an appeasement to God's wrath ascends in the order from the least valuable to the most valuable . . . burnt offerings, calves, rams, rivers of oil, and eventually the first-born son. The religious offenders in Micah are willing to give everything in their possession, including their children, as a sacrifice. However, they are unwilling to give themselves in the practice of justice and mercy toward their neighbor. Israel thinks that sharing material commodities *with God* will excuse them from the divine wrath aroused by their incredulous acts of injustice *against human beings*.

Israel's list of possible offerings consists of material goods that Hebrew society highly values. They assume that Yahweh places the same value on these commodities. But they soon discover that their value system is totally different from God's value system. Hebrew society values religious commodities. Yahweh values compassionate community.

Yahweh cannot be bribed into excusing the blatant injustice that's practiced in Israel. He is not impressed by the religious offerings of material things that he already owns as creator. And neither is God impressed with the commercial goods and commodities that are highly esteemed in the American society.

Christians must ask the question, What does the Lord really require of the American church today? What are the commercial goods on our list of possible offerings that we use to appease God's wrath against the church's silence in the face of American injustice?

God is not impressed with the fancy upgrades we make in his name to the church buildings that provide shelter for our sanctimonies and ceremonial sacrifices.

One church in Dallas is presently building a massive structure. The pastor, leading the fundraising charge, explains, "As I look around downtown Dallas, I see spectacular temples of commerce, of culture and of government—many new, some restored to former glory, and all intended to stand for generations. The Kingdom of God needs a home to equal them—a spiritual oasis in the middle of downtown."

The church's Web site justifies the cost of such gigantic undertaking by comparing the cost of this campus to other recent downtown Dallas construction projects. "It will cost in the $130 million range, substantially less than the Convention Center Hotel (an expected $500 million) and the Dallas Center for the Performing Arts ($354 million), both worthy projects. We expect our new sanctuary to take its rightful place alongside them as a world-class facility."

An affluent society is probably impressed with new buildings and temples that are spectacular in architecture and design. However, despite the fact that Christians live in an affluent society, the church in America must continue to ask the critical question, "What does the Lord require?"

- "What does the Lord require?" Does the Lord require that Christians spend $130 million dollars on construct-

ing a church plant to compete with the kingdoms of this world, or does God require that Christians spend the money to bring mercy and compassion to South Dallas?
- "What does the Lord require?" Does the Lord require that Christians spend $130 million dollars on facilities that will provide shelter for church activities, or does God require that Christians spend the money to provide affordable housing for families that have been displaced by a global economic meltdown?
- "What does the Lord require?" Does the Lord require that Christians spend $130 million dollars on "world-class facilities," or does God require Christians to spend the money to bring justice and compassion in the workplace for immigrant workers who are being mercilessly exploited?
- "What does the Lord require?" Does the Lord desire costly buildings, or provisions for the high cost of college tuition for children from low income families?
- "What does the Lord require?"

No matter how beautifully constructed our assembly houses are, they cannot distract God's attention from the injustices that worshippers actively or passively allow to be practiced against the poor. Yahweh makes clear his requirements in Isaiah 58.

God says,

> Yet on the day of your fasting, you do as you please and exploit all your workers. Your fasting ends in quarreling and strife, and in striking each other with wicked fists. You cannot fast as you do today and expect your voice to be heard on high.... Is not this kind of fasting I have chosen: to loose the chains of injustice and untie the cords of the yoke, to set the oppressed free and break every yoke? Is it not to share your food with the

hungry and to provide the poor wanderer with shelter—when you see the naked, to clothe him, and not turn away from your own flesh and blood?

In this text's prophetic shadow, Micah says, "He has showed you, O man, what is good" (6:8).

- "What is good?" Good is when you act justly toward your neighbor!
- "What is good?" Good is when you loose the chains of injustice by not cheating poor undocumented workers out of their hard-earned wages.
- "What is good?" Good is when you untie the cords of the yoke of disproportionate unemployment among those living in our major inner cities.
- "What is good?" Good is when you set the oppressed free from the mental shackles of miseducation placed on them by a failed public school system.
- "What is good?" Good is when you break every yoke of violence that hate groups perpetrate against people of color.
- "What is good?" Good is when you show mercy by providing food for the poor in the Appalachians and in the Mississippi Delta.

Micah has established the solid case that God requires Israel to turn its attention away from the material commodities of society and to think upon what is required to create a more just and compassionate community. Micah is making the case that love, compassion, righteousness, and mercy must become Israel's only "public option." Church programs as well as governmental policies must be rooted in justice and grounded in compassion if they are to have a transformative effect upon the nation.

- If we speak in the tongues of men and of angels but do not "do justice" and do not "love kindness," it is only a resounding gong and a clanging cymbal.
- If we come before God with all our burnt offerings or with ten thousand rivers of oil but do not "do justice" and do not "love kindness," it means nothing.
- If we come before God with our professional praise teams and our meticulously planned worship services, but do not "do justice" and do not "love kindness," it means nothing!
- If we come before God with our polished sermons and amazing testimonies, but do not "do justice" and do not "love kindness," it means nothing!

The Lord desires mercy and not sacrifices (Hosea 6:6). He does not desire religion driven by Lucifer's principle of pride and arrogance. In Micah, arrogance struts through the streets of Israel, marching to the loud music of foolish pride. Pride is at the very root of social injustice. Pride says, "I don't have to respect the rights of others; I simply take from others whatever I want and am strong enough to take." Pride is narcissistic; it thinks the whole world revolves around its agenda.

Pride thinks it has an entitlement to capitalize on the weaknesses of third-world poverty. Pride thinks it has the right to bring poor migrant workers into the United States from Latin America to do hard labor at slave wages. Narcissistic pride has the audacity to call the migrant workers illegal without identifying the illegal businesses that brought them here with the intent to exploit them!

The church must not remain silent in the face of such prideful injustices. The church must be God's mouthpiece in a world that is taken captive by selfish greed. Let us not become like the people described in Ezekiel 16:49. Ezekiel says that "the entire nation is arrogant, overfed and has no concern for the poor."

Let us follow the prophetic example of Micah. Micah, being a country prophet, speaks for the poor farmers who are suffering at the hands of powerful landlords. Micah sees greedy men unmercifully dispossessing the poor and corrupt leaders fearlessly standing in the way of justice like an iron gate. He says "the powerful lay awake at night devising wickedness."

The church must not remain passive in the face of such mentalities that act in blatant aggression against the poor. We are called to walk "humbly" before our God. Our "humble" concern for the poor will become a countercultural reality that subverts any social order that builds itself upon the foundations of pride and arrogance.

Micah reminds us in 6:8 that the Lord requires that we walk humbly with him as we also walk humbly with the vulnerable in our midst. God does not desire dead animals on the altar; he desires living hearts that with humility place themselves upon the altar of love for the neighbor.

- He wants humble hearts attached to feet that will walk for justice with the underprivileged on the streets of Dallas, Detroit, Los Angeles, and Memphis.
- He wants humble hearts attached to feet that will walk for justice with disenfranchised farmers in the rural areas across America.
- He wants humble hearts attached to feet that walk for justice with migrant farm workers in North Carolina and California.
- He wants humble hearts that motivate feet to walk for justice with undocumented workers who are being treated unjustly in America's poultry industry.
- When we walk humbly with God, it means that we see ourselves connected to something greater and more important than our own puny egos.

- When we walk humbly with God, our inner attachment with God's feelings causes us to care about the people that God cares about; our emotional alliance with God's emotions prevents us from acting unjustly towards other human beings.
- When we walk humbly with God, it frees us from the rat race of self-promotion, heartless competition and the desire to be number one in everything; we desist from meeting arrogant pride with arrogant pride.
- As humble servants of God, we are no longer enslaved to the idea of doing evil for evil, dropping bomb for bomb, firing missile for missile, and rendering attack for attack.
- When we walk humbly with God, we perfectly understand that evil is never conquered by the use of evil. We learn that the only power that is greater than evil is good.
- Walking humbly with God teaches us how to build community around a vision of compassion, instead of around a hateful vision of violence inspired by the doctrines of seducing spirits.
- Walking humbly with God builds the church into a holy nation wherein we become the house of prayer for all nations.
- Walking humbly with God will lead us step by step to that well-lit city of love, mercy, and justice.
  - Our feet might get tired, but we will keep stepping.
  - Our courage may become dizzy, but we will keep walking.
  - Our vision of the bright-lit city may grow dim, but we will keep marching until we sit in that place wherein every knee is bowed to the Christ and every tongue confesses his name.

So, let us walk together children, and don't get weary, because there is a great camp meeting in the Promised Land filled with justice, love, and compassion. This is what the Lord requires!

WHAT DOES THE LORD REQUIRE?

A Critical Biblical Response

Walter Brueggemann

In this sermon, Jerry Taylor takes up a familiar prophetic text and shows the way in which the text is an immediate contemporary summons to us.

I.

What I like most about the sermon is the way in which Taylor develops powerful rhetorical riffs from the words of Micah. There are spectacular examples of this in the sermon.

First, in Micah 6:5 the prophet calls Israel to remember and in verse 4 enunciates the memory of the Exodus. From that Taylor develops a series, "remember the journey," by which he walks the congregation through the definitive biblical material. He then easily glides over into more contemporary matters concerning the wars, military buildup, and the recent economic meltdown. All of these memories, he makes clear, are of a piece.

Second, he plays from the phrase, "'walk humbly with God," and offers a series of evangelical demands, each of which requires a decision against the ailments of our society. My only disappointment here is that I think the preacher missed an opportunity to develop parallel series of rhetorical points on the other phrases of Micah, "do justice" and "love kindness." He hints at these, but they do not receive such full development. If he had offered parallel sequences to these two phrases, this would have been the meat of an even richer sermon. The practice of such powerful, relentless patterns of speech is a peculiar feature of African American preaching, a practice from which we white preachers are learning, albeit slowly, that the sermon is indeed a rhetorical performance. In these two instances, Taylor exhibits a remarkable capacity to take the conversation into the heart of the claim of the text.

In other instances he offers the same technique, some even more fully developed. He offers a series of questions that God may ask indicted Israel, "Did I offend you ...?" And at the end of the sermon he has a wondrous triad of "feet, courage, vision," that builds from the concrete to the soaring summons, "We will keep marching." All of this is powerful stuff that recruits the attention and the resolve of the congregation.

II.

I also like how quickly the sermon gets to the text. My own bias is that the preacher must get to the text promptly, because the text is more compelling and more interesting than most of what else we might say. The longer the text is delayed in the sermon, the greater chance we have of "losing the audience." In this sermon we are immediately oriented to the social context assumed and defined in the entirety of Micah through Taylor's paraphrased but quick litany, ".... price gouging ... corrupt trading practices ... unregulated greed ... false weights ... rigged measurements." The collection of sins, drawn from the larger prophetic text, provides immediate moorings for the sermon to make cultural and modern connections, allowing the congregation to sail into active, missional engagement. The voice of the rural poet in the text speaks on behalf of abused peasants and claims a kind of compelling authority that more abstract theorists never attain.

III.

I applaud the sermon's concrete connections between text and contemporaneity, so that the question of "God's requirement" becomes available to the congregation. In the general survey of Micah, the preacher makes many credible connections. It is important, in my judgment, to provide specific textual references for the details of the poet, and to linger over the wording of the text itself. The sermon immediately sets up these relations through analogy ("like the rising flood waters of Hurricane Katrina"), contrast (Israel's "pledge of allegiance"), and direct comparison ("A similar practice is carried on by some American companies")—all within the sermon's first minute! There is no doubt to this sermon's direction and authority.

I think the contrast between the inventory of verses 6-7 and that of verse 8 is clear and sharp. It is often noticed that the list of possible (and rejected) offerings moves from the least valuable to the most valuable . . . burnt offerings, calves, rams, rivers of oil, and eventually first-born son. All of these are treated as valuable *commodities*. By contrast, the three famous phrases of verse 8 are all about *relationships* or, if one wants a "c" word to go along with commodity, *communion*. Thus the choice before Israel—and before the congregation—is *commodity or relationship, commodity or communion*. The pressure in our society to choose commodity is immense, as it was in ancient Israel. The prophet, and now the preacher, knows "a more excellent way." The sermon exploits this opportunity to think through the process of choosing relationships and resisting commodities, first with Taylor's observation, "Israel thinks that sharing material commodities *with God* will excuse them from the divine wrath aroused by their incredulous acts of injustice *against human beings*," then with clarification, "Hebrew society values religious commodities. Yahweh values compassionate community," then connecting the worlds into one, "And, neither is God impressed with the commercial goods and commodities that are highly esteemed in the American society," and finally with the closing bevy of answers to the single question, "What does the Lord require?" This is more than rhetorical flourish. Taylor models with biblical precision the summons of the text, which is to engage in genuinely countercultural activity. That is how it always was in ancient Israel, as it always is now in the church.

4

The Legacy of Queen Vashti

Compositional Notes

This sermon was delivered February 22, 2005 at the Abilene Christian University Lectureship for the annual Men's Fellowship Banquet where the audience of about four hundred were predominately southern white males who serve as congregational ministers or elders.

As I spent time absorbing the text in Esther 4:10-17, I realized that though women were physically absent, Queen Vashti would be the one female who would figure prominently in the male consciousness on this occasion. I thought that a banquet based on gender would be a very fitting opportunity to speak to the issue of gender discrimination that often happens at the hands of men who are in high places of positional power.

Many of the Christian men attending the banquet were very successful businessmen. Some had personal friendships with President

George W. Bush and others had direct access to the Bush administration. In 2005 conservative Evangelicals probably felt more connected to George W. Bush than they did to any other president since Ronald Reagan. The banquet served as an opportunity to ask Christian men to think about how they use their access to power on behalf of women and others who have historically been denied power in American society.

The role of women in the church was a very hot topic of debate in 2005 among many Churches of Christ. In some conservative Churches of Christ women have been historically treated as second-class citizens. The increased visibility of women participating in public worship had caused some churches to split. Because this was such a divisive issue in the church, most church leaders were overtaken by a spirit of fear and refused to address the issue in their local congregation. As I developed the sermon, it was my hope that it would serve as a prophetic word to elders, ministers, and other leaders in local churches encouraging them to stop the repression and oppression of our sisters.

In the sermon I seek to make the case that brave-hearted men are in great demand when it comes to standing up and confronting injustice against women in the church and society. The legacy of Queen Vashti is a living indictment against all men who live in fear!

THE LEGACY OF QUEEN VASHTI

Esther 4:10-17

Fear is the filibuster that stalls the debate over whether or not Christian men should use their influence to encourage the righteous use of power within the social and political arrangements of society.

- Fear is the crippling disease that causes Christian leaders to suffer a stroke in the muscles of their moral courage, leaving them with a deformed and twisted commitment to the compassionate use of their God-given influence.
- Fear is the seductive mentor of cowards who train Christian men how to cleverly occupy the office of power without teaching them how to exercise the authority of the office to influence the promotion of a compassionate agenda on behalf of the powerless in our world.
- Fear has given some Christian men an attachment to their high positions on the great mountain of prestige, allowing them to ignore the pitiful plight of their brothers and sisters who are drowning in the muddy waters of misery in the flood zones of unjustifiable injustice.

Some Christian leaders have swallowed the idea that it is morally right for them to use their influence to promote righteousness within the social structures of society. But, after having swallowed this moral idea, many Christian leaders have attempted to rinse it down with the sour wine of fear, which has given them a serious case of ethical indigestion. Christian leaders must see fear as a terminally ill pet that must be put to sleep. Fear must no longer be permitted to walk around on an unguarded leash, barking discouragement into the hearts of godly men.

Christian leaders must recognize fear as the immoral mortician that directs them to turn their chairs away from their corporate windows, ignoring the funeral procession of a dead hope that has been lynched on a thousand trees in the orchard of global greed and international politics.

- Let us, as Christian men, refuse to permit fear to hold our moral courage hostage any longer.
- Let us find the courage to summon divine authority to escort fear from the premises of our hearts, and
- let us have fear arrested as an unlawful intruder.
- Let us, as Christian leaders, bravely declare that our integrity is no longer for sale.
- Let us boldly declare that we are no longer pledging for membership in the fraternity of cowards.

As Christian leaders, we know the difference between prophets and professional politicians. Prophets promote God's merciful agenda in the world, while professional politicians promote the expansion of their own political careers. Prophets carry within themselves the burden of speaking the truth in love, while professional politicians speak only those things that will enhance their positions of prestige and honor, assuring their entitlement to unlimited political perks, pleasures, and benefits.

The narrative in Esther chapter 1 shows us clearly the relationship between the king and his professional politicians. We are given a glimpse into how favorably King Xerxes treated his high-ranking officials who conformed to his will. We are also given a glimpse into the moral failure of the professional politicians who failed to hold the king accountable for his unjust actions and abuse of power.

The king called together to Susa, the capital city of the Persian Empire, all of his high-ranking officials for a seven-day feast in the court of the garden of the king's palace. These powerful men made up an elite political network that had direct access to the machinery of government within the Persian Empire that dominated the global geopolitical landscape of that time. The elite men attending this gala were the privileged who could now say they had made it completely inside the Beltway of the Persian political establishment. Having access to this high-powered gathering was a lobbyist's paradise.

The king appealed to the spirit of consumerism and materialism in his elite men by exposing them to the lavish interior designs of the palace garden. The palace garden decorations sensually appealed to the lust of the eye, the lust of the flesh, and the pride of life. Some scholars believe that the purpose of this display of royal grandeur was to inspire the Persians with confidence in preparation for the massive—and ultimately disastrous—military campaign against Greece (the only significant part of the world known to Xerxes not under his control). The Palace Garden had hangings of white and blue linen, fastened with cords of white linen and purple material with silver rings on marble pillars. There were couches of gold and silver on a mosaic pavement of porphyry, marble, mother-of pearl, and other costly stones. The wine was served in golden goblets, each one with its own unique design.

The king made sure that, on this festive occasion, there was an abundance of royal wine. He shared the abundance of his wine with his elite men as a token of his generosity toward those who had proven their loyalty and support to his throne, which extended from Asia Minor down into Africa and across the northern parts of India. The king passed a law at this event that deregulated the consumption of the royal wine among the elite men; the stewards were instructed to serve each man the amount of wine he desired. The king's elite men readily participated in this deregulated spirit of consumerism. The abundant supply of royal wine was the symbol of Persian affluence and wealth.

In this consumer-driven gathering of the Persian political elite, we are given a glimpse of an ancient practice of gender segregation. While the king entertained the male guests in the court of the palace, Queen Vashti occupied their wives in the royal house. These two gender segregated groups were both separate and unequal.

- One group had direct access to political power, while the other group had, at best, a secondary access.
- One group was dominant, while the other group was subordinate.
- One group was classified as superior, while the other group was categorized as inferior.
- One group consisted of the insiders, while the other group consisted of the outsiders.

This is often the type of disparity that exists when groups are not genuinely integrated on the firm basis of total inclusion.

According to the narrative, on the seventh day the king's heart became lively with wine; the king had become a victim of his own policy of unrestricted consumerism. Under the influence of his own royal wine, he sent seven chamberlains to the group of females with the royal order to bring Queen Vashti before the king with her royal regalia. She was to be added to his other exhibits that he had placed on public display. The king had already impressed his male guests with the beautiful allurements of his palace, now he wished to impress them with the beautiful appearance of his queen, for the text says, "she was lovely to look at." The spirit of consumerism unleashed in the king's palace had overtaken the king to the point he was attempting to consume the human dignity of his own wife.

The king's action suggests that, within the Persian society, it was culturally acceptable for women to be used as sexual commodities for public consumption, indulging the sensual appetite of lustful men. Scholars believe that during this historical period it was a customary practice on such festive occasions for the kings to show off the physical beauty of their queens. There are dehumanizing customs in the history of all nations. However, I believe that, no matter how long a national habit has been entrenched within the fabric of a society or institution, there is never justification for the maintenance of any traditional custom or ideology that degrades the humanity of another human being.

Queen Vhasti had to give her response to this unjust demand. If she refused the king's demand, she could lose everything she had, including her life. The queen could have decided to suffer this grave injustice in order to hold on to her first lady status. She could have decided that bearing the degrading insult was more tolerable than parting with her attachment to the comfort and security of the king's palace. She could have decided that the political perks were more valuable to her than the dignity of her humanity.

Queen Vhasti took a risk. She made a decision to act with integrity in the face of invasive power. The king's response to Vashti's decision was one of violent anger. Vashti's action exposed the autocratic, tyrannical, dictatorial, and authoritarian spirit of the king. Xerxes is characterized by the ancient Greek historian Herodotus as being impatient, hot-tempered, and lecherous. The king would not permit anyone, including his own wife, to publicly disagree with him. This attitude revealed that his power had become self-serving and abusive. Political power and earthly authority can lead swiftly down the winding road of pride and arrogance. Those fortunate enough to hold power in the left hand must balance it with wisdom and humility in the right hand, and both hands must know what the other is doing at all times!

The king viewed everything in Persia as belonging to him. Verse 7 speaks of "the royal wine," verse 18 speaks of "the king's nobles," and verse 22 speaks of his royal provinces. Everything and everyone existed for the purpose and use of the king. No one dared to disobey the king, but Vashti did. The queen's refusal to comply with the king's command disturbed the court festivities. Vashti refused to participate any further in the shallow, self-congratulatory actions of the king. Her refusal to bow down to the king's command foreshadowed Mordecai's refusal to bow down to Haman's demand to be worshiped in Esther 4.

Although the king was in a fit of rage, he was wise enough to ask his elite men to advise him on how he should respond to Vashti's perceived act of rebellion. The elite men were in a strategic advisory position with an opportunity to rightly and wisely influence the king to use his power and force with wisdom, patience, and compassion.

I wonder how Christian leaders would have advised the king had we been in this advisory position. I wonder if our advice would have been different from that of the elite men in our narrative. Would Christian leaders' advice be based upon the love ethic of Jesus, or would it be based on the sinful nature's need to manipulate, dominate, and control?

In verse 18, Me-mu-can advises the king by saying, "This very day the Persian and Median women of the nobility who have heard about the queen's conduct will respond to all the king's nobles in the same way. There will be no end of disrespect and discord." In essence, he said to the king that, if you allow your wife to defend herself against your mistreatment and disrespect, it will cause our wives to disrespect us as men. Me-mu-can advised the king that the best domestic policy for dealing with a potential woman's resistance movement in the Persian kingdom is to crush the leader of it with a decisive blow. Make it clear to all the women in the kingdom that any resistance to the inhumane and demoralizing treatment of women will be met with immediate and decisive force. No female dissent will be allowed!

Me-mu-can's advice to the king was not based on justice and righteousness, but it was based on the protection of the self-interests of his own group. Me-mu-can had the king's ear, but fear and selfishness had Me-mu-can's heart, which prevented him from advising the king to shape his domestic agenda according to righteous judgment. As men of God, let us not promote the interests of our particular group when those interests work to the detriment of the life and dignity of other human beings. According to Me-mu-can's advice, a domestic policy was passed and could not be repealed. Vashti was never again to enter the presence of King Xerxes. She was terminated from her position for insubordination, and she was labeled as a rabble-rouser. Her position was given to someone else that the king determined was better than she, someone who would surrender to the inhumane treatment of women.

The king's domestic agenda has passed the Persian house and senate, legislating that every man should rule in his own house. But, we stand here today as Christian men of God, whose hearts have been touched by Jesus. We seek to make a provision to that bill. Men of God believe that men should rule well their own houses, but we rule with the provision of love, tenderness, patience, humility, boldness, firmness, courage, justice, fairness, truth, and righteousness. As Christian leaders sitting around the royal conference tables of our day, let us give godly input into the shaping of agendas, realizing that these decisions will have a far-reaching impact upon everyone on the planet. As men of God, let us be diligent in our efforts to influence political powers to be just and fair in the domestic and international decisions that will affect the most vulnerable and weak in our society and world.

As Christian leaders, we no longer give our consent to any custom, law, or policy that serves to the detriment of human dignity in people at home or abroad. As men of God, we pray for the courageous boldness that will be dressed in the attire of love and humility and will empower us to speak not what is politically popular, but to speak what is morally right. Let us give support to the voices of the defenseless, the vulnerable, the children, the elderly, the aliens, and the oppressed. Let us resist the temptation to distance ourselves from the public discourse taking place in the marketplace of our times. Let us remain politically engaged, offering a critical voice in the discussion and adding the compassionate spirit of our Savior to the political dialogue.

As men of God, we stand against abortion, the killing of babies before they are born, and *we also stand* for a domestic policy that serves to sustain the health and quality of life for babies after they have been born. We not only want to see babies delivered into the world, but we also want to see them delivered from the stubborn grips of poverty and neglect.

As men of God, we stand against crime and criminality on all levels, but *we also stand* for the genuine rehabilitation of prisoners and the offering of communal forgiveness and embrace, especially to those converted to Jesus, now released from prison and seeking to make a new start.

As men of God, we are against laziness and the unwillingness to work, but *we are also* for the fair treatment of migrant workers who do hard labor in industries that cleverly practice a new and improved form of slavery.

As men of God, we believe in being subject to the governing authorities, but *we also believe* that we must not remain silent whenever we witness falsehood, dishonesty, and deception having a field day on the sacred fairgrounds of truth.

As men of God, we are committed to doing our humble duty wherever God stations us, but *we are also committed* to accepting the risk of being evicted from our positions of prestige, status, and power in order to promote the righteous reign of God almighty wherever we are.

There is no greater position than the position God has reserved for all his children, who have their robes washed in the blood of the lamb and who traverse through the bloody trenches of trials and tribulations desperately hungering for God's righteousness to be done on earth as it is in heaven. As Christian leaders positioned around the tables of power at the king's invitation, let us not be afraid to speak as God's representatives.

Let us not be the Sauls of the twenty-first century, standing by and quietly holding the political cloaks of those driven by arrogance and greed and who blindly stone to death the weak and defenseless in our world, for we sit at the table of that heavenly king who owns earth and sky. He has whispered into our ears the battle cry that "it is time to speak and act with courage!" Let us not fear the consequences of doing what is morally right in God's sight, but let us fear the consequences of doing what is morally popular in the sight of men. Our courage has been unchained, and our tongues have been set free to speak and sing of the loving righteousness of a king who sits high and looks low. Men of God, this is not the time to be afraid. When we fear the king of heaven, we fear no kings of worldly stature.

- Psalms 27:1, 3 says, "The LORD is my light and my salvation—whom shall I fear? The LORD is the stronghold of my life—of whom shall I be afraid? Though an army besiege me, my heart will not fear; though war break out against me, even then will I be confident."
- Isaiah 41:13 says, "For I am the LORD, your God, who takes hold of your right hand and says to you, Do not fear; I will help you."
- Isaiah 51:12 says, "I, even I, am he who comforts you. Who are you that you fear mortal men, the sons of men who are but grass?"
- 2 Timothy 1:7 says, "For God did not give us the spirit of timidity, but of power, of love and of self-discipline."
- Hebrews 13:6 says, "So we say with confidence, the Lord is my helper: I will not be afraid. What can man do to me?"

"THE LEGACY OF QUEEN VASHTI"

A Theological and Homiletical Response

Ronald Allen

This brief response first comments on how this sermon—coming from the book of Esther—is prophetic. I then call attention to some qualities of the sermon that provide models for other preachers. The essay concludes by articulating a modest reservation.

When I was much younger, I thought of prophetic preaching as angry confrontation. The prophet—outraged by idolatry, exploitation, injustice, and violence—would confront the congregation with its unfaithfulness, and threaten the congregation with doom if the people did not repent. Over the years, I have come to recognize that the prophet is, instead, a kind of ombudsperson who helps the community reflect on the degree to which the community is living in accord with the covenant (God's purposes). The prophet identifies points at which the community strays towards unfaithfulness. The prophet aims to help the community recognize its unfaithfulness and to take remedial action both to avoid condemnation and to return to a life of blessing.

We usually associate prophetic sermons with preaching from the prophets. However, a preacher can speak prophetically from any book of the Bible when helping the community assess its faithfulness along the lines described above. The book of Esther is not, technically, a prophetic book but a Writing. Although Esther does not belong to the genre of prophecy, Professor Taylor makes prophetic use of the book by helping the church today reflect critically on the degree to which we are faithful to God's purposes in public life, in the congregation, and in the home. This sermon, then, is instructive not only in its own right but as a model for preaching prophetically from parts of the Bible that are not technically in the prophets.

When thinking about other ways in which the sermon might inspire a preacher today, I must call attention to Professor Taylor's provocative use of language. Every single paragraph contains turns of phrase, images, and descriptions that arrest the imagination. The sentences in this homily are straightforward, with verbs in the active voice. This style helps the listener immediately understand the point and feel directly addressed.

At the outset, the sermon names one of the biggest obstacles to prophetic living: fear. Many people in congregations are afraid to "promote God's merciful agenda in the world." However, in a masterful mode of communication, the preacher does not berate listeners for being afraid but approaches their fear empathetically, thus establishing identification between preacher and congregation. The community, then, is willing to go with the preacher into the rest of the sermon.

The heart of the homily uses the story of Vashti as a lens for helping the church recognize how we envision and use power. Are we like Xerxes—accumulating and using power for our own self-serving ends, even when these ends disrupt God's purposes and bring about suffering and death? Or are we like Vashti—taking the risk of defying the Xerxeses of this world to witness to God's intent for all to experience respect, dignity, acceptance, justice, community, and abundance?

In the last part of the sermon, Professor Taylor directly helps the congregation consider how to make prophetic witness in specific situations in life. Homiletically, this is the most brilliant part of the sermon. The preacher first names a point on which nearly all listeners would agree, and then makes a logical extension of that point into an area of life which the listeners might not have considered or about which they might be uneasy. For example, not only should we be against "laziness and unwillingness to work" but we should stand for "the fair treatment of migrant workers who do hard labor in industries that cleverly practice a new and improved form of slavery." The preacher implies, "If you listeners agree with my first point here, you will surely agree with the second." This approach works not by in-your-face confrontation (which often generates defensiveness, hostility, and rejection) but by inviting listeners to consider where their values naturally lead.

This sermon manifests integrity between the preacher and the message. While Professor Taylor encourages *the congregation* to be courageous by standing for God's purposes for all of God's children, *this sermon itself* is a risk. For some people both in and out of the church oppose—even violently—some of the values central to this message.

Of course, when interpreting God's purposes for today, different communities sometimes come to different conclusions. I imagine that the community in which Professor Taylor preached this sermon shared with him the conviction that terminating pregnancy is wrong (except under circumstances that would save the life of the mother). Some Christians view this situation differently on theological grounds—and not simply as a matter of political correctness or convenience. While I appreciate the sermon's insistence that standing against terminating pregnancy should also mean standing for "domestic policy that serves to sustain the health and quality of life," I wish that emphasis had been extended to standing against capital punishment (an ultimate form of disrespect). Of course, a finite preacher cannot cover the almost infinite list of topics that could be mentioned in such a sermon.

This reservation is minor when viewed from the larger task of this sermon. When empowered by the Holy Spirit, sermons in the stream of this one can help congregations turn away from ways they live short of God's intentions and take steps towards cooperating with God's purposes, thereby increasing dignity, respect, health, quality of life, fair treatment, safety, health, and courage. That is a legacy worthy not only of Queen Vashti but of the One who has washed our robes in his own blood.

5

Christmas According to Matthew

Compositional Notes

This message was presented as a Christmas sermon on December 16, 2007 at the Highland Church of Christ in Abilene, Texas, in the midst of my 2005 to 2008 tenure as the associate minister. I shared pulpit responsibilities with Mike Cope and continue to maintain relationship with the congregation through interim preaching and regular worship.

Matthew 2:1-18 addresses both the tragic and joyful experiences that surround Jesus' birth which occurs in a political and religious environment filled with competitive power struggles and religious rivalry. In such a world, those who have the power are bent on maintaining it by any means necessary. Herod proves his willingness to kill anyone who is perceived as a threat to his throne. The proof of his ruthlessness is seen in his murderous decisions that led to the destruction of innocent children.

The point is made early in the sermon that Herod embodies the spirit of death while Jesus embodies the spirit of life. It is necessary in light of the overarching point of the sermon to describe how the same struggle between life and death continues today even in the midst of a joyful Christmas season. The description of this struggle seeks to discourage the audience from being uninformed participants in a national Christmas festival that distorts the significant truth embedded within Jesus' birth narrative. Christmas according to Matthew is about something much more significant than trees and presents.

In Herod's attempt to destroy Jesus in 2:4, he seeks intelligence about Jesus' whereabouts by turning to the religious leaders. Herod is portrayed as a deceptive pretender who gives the false impression that he is a true worshiper of the Christ child. It is here that the text enables me to make the audience aware of the ongoing saga of worldly powers that continue to exploit organized religion. The powerful of this world, under the guise of worshiping Christ, still engage in using religion in ways that benefit them politically and economically.

I end the Christmas sermon by using the phrase "the Herod spirit" as a rhetorical device that enables me to critique today's contemporary entities that continue to exploit the birth of Jesus. It also allows me to critique a Christmas materialism that believes genuine affection for loved ones is measured by the price and number of gifts given to them on Christmas day.

CHRISTMAS ACCORDING TO MATTHEW

Matthew 2:1-18

According to Matthew, Magi from the east wisely discover that something special has happened upon the earth in the vicinity of Jerusalem. Their star-gazing guides them to the city of Jerusalem, wherein they ask the question, "Where is the one who has been born king of the Jews? We saw his star in the east and have come to worship him." When the wise students of the night sky published their reading of the constellations, Herod and all Jerusalem with him become *disturbed*.

I would think that the Magi's announcement should bring great joy to Israel, but, instead of the people rejoicing, they become fearfully *unsettled*.

- Isn't it still true that people don't recognize good news when they hear it?
- Isn't it still true that powerful people in high places are *disturbed* when they hear of the birth of an heir to their thrones?

Herod decides that only one sheriff can wear the star in his town. The announcement of Christ's birth signals a potential rival to Herod's throne, and Herod will do whatever is necessary to secure his kingship.

According to Matthew, the morning star appears on the scene, and now both Herod's political standing and the Jewish religious establishment stand to lose their stellar status and become falling and fading stars descending from the canopy of heaven. Herod, in all of his political might and human wisdom, seeks to restrain the will of God and to obstruct the hand of destiny. His great status fills his head with the prideful notion that he has the infinite power to orchestrate and manipulate the unfolding of events taking place in heaven and on earth.

In his haste to take preventive measures against the rising star of Christ, Herod assembles a religious think tank consisting of chief priests and teachers of the law. Herod uses the religious leaders of Israel to get information to destroy the Messiah, the promised one of Israel. Instead of the religious leaders seeking to protect the Christ from the fearful king, they give him intelligence that could potentially enable him to destroy the Christ child before he reaches manhood.

Often, organized religion betrays Christ to the corrupt political intentions of Herod, who kills and destroys all in his way to strengthen his grip on power in a global economy. Despotic rulers of this age have always resisted and sought to sabotage the royal entrance of the king of heaven into the world that he has made. The human creature's darkness is so thick that he is compelled to snuff out any potential light that might cause him to see himself as a limited creature vainly seeking the status of a god.

Herod thinks that his will is more powerful than God's will in this world, and his spoiling surroundings of pomp, pageantry, and circumstance give him the deceptive idea that he is more than what he really is. Herod commits the folly of thinking more highly of himself than he should, therefore deceiving himself. According to Matthew, Herod thinks that he can preserve his political power by killing the God-sent Christ child. According to historians, Herod was so obsessed with preserving his kingship that he had some of his own family members killed when he thought they posed a threat to his throne.

Herod questions the religious leaders by asking them, "Where was the Christ to be born?" They give Herod the intelligence he is searching for by telling him exactly what the prophet has written; they tell him that Christ is to be born in Bethlehem in Judea. So, Herod has a secret meeting with the Magi to discern the exact time the star appeared. He tells them to go to Bethlehem and make a careful search for the child and, as soon as they find him, to report back so that he too may go and worship him.

Matthew portrays Herod as a deceptive pretender. Herod gives the false impression that he is a true worshiper of the Christ child. He thinks that the Magi are unsuspecting of his true motives and are willing to go along with his deceptive and deadly plan that intends to bring about the death of the Christ child in Bethlehem. We are told that the star the Magi had seen in the east "went ahead of them until it stopped over the place where the child was."

When they saw the star, they were overjoyed and felt they had found what they had been searching for. How do we feel this morning when we see the star? Some people get excited over Hollywood stars like Tom Cruise, Will Smith, or Halle Berry. I've never seen a movie star that makes me want to shout the way I want to shout whenever I behold the star of the Christ child. Movie stars get their star put into a sidewalk in Hollywood to be walked upon, but the Christ child has a star in heaven to be gazed upon.

Matthew tells us that, upon coming to the house, the Magi see the child with his mother, Mary, and according to the custom in the ancient east, they bow down and worship him. They open their treasures and present him with gifts of gold, incense, and myrrh. Such overwhelming joy among the Magi results in unrestricted praise and worship and the giving of gifts to the Christ child.

We too rejoice today, feel great excitement about the Christ and want to give to him. We too open our treasures and give gifts of gold, incense, and myrrh.

- We see this Christ child all around us today in the form of mutilated bodies that have been deformed by war and famine.
- We see the Christ child in the sunken eyes of those hungry souls being ethnically cleansed in the Sudan.
- We see the Christ child in the form of every person on the homeless streets of America who says to us during

> this season to "be jolly, when I was hungry you fed me, when I was thirsty you gave me something to drink, when I was in prison you visited me and when I was naked you clothed me."

We pour out our gifts not upon ourselves, but upon the Christ child when we encounter him in the form of the little children who face abuse and abandonment. This is the season to search the sky for the stars of orphans and neglected widows forgotten in orphanages and nursing homes.

After the wise men worship the child Jesus, they are warned in a dream not to go back to Herod, and they return to their country by another route. Joseph is told in a dream to take the child and his mother and escape to Egypt and that Herod is going to search for the child to kill him.

Herod's spirit is still on the loose today. It seeks to kill the hope and aspirations in the eye of every child born in poverty, and it seeks to crush the dreams of children by leaving them trapped in a permanent underclass wherein they are prepared to be warehoused products in the prison system for life.

Will our joy for the Christ child sustain us to give gifts this Christmas season to those who feel starless? The Christ child is always in the company of the children who live in poverty. The Christ child who had a star in the heavens did not even have a room in which to be born. His mother gave birth to him in a station of poverty.

The Magi are warned in a dream not to go back to Herod, and they return to their country by another route. The Magi decide not to turn the Christ child in to Herod. Herod is furious when he realizes that he has been outwitted by the wise men. So, he gives orders to kill all the boys in Bethlehem and its vicinity who were two years old and under in accordance with the information he had from the Magi.

This massacre of children is similar to when the Egyptians feared that the Israelites were numerically outgrowing them. In the midst of the massacre in Egypt, Moses' life was preserved by Pharaoh's daughter. Matthew shows the irony in that the future of Israel, symbolized in the Christ child, has to be taken into Egypt for safety and protection from his own people in Jerusalem. The promised Messiah has to be taken into the very land from which his people had been delivered. The land of bondage becomes the land of refuge. As Moses' life was preserved in Pharaoh's palace until he was of age to lead his people to the Promised Land, so too is Jesus' life preserved in Egypt until he is no longer threatened by the murderous King Herod.

Herod's spirit is still alive today. Herod's spirit seeks to destroy the innocent lives of children in sweat shops and forced child labor camps all over the world.

- Will we refuse to cooperate or collaborate?
- Will we protect the Christ children in our midst from when Herod's spirit forces their poor parents to remain in poverty?
- Will we withhold fair wages for their hard labor?
- Will we protect the Christ children in our society when Herod's spirit seeks to abort their precious lives before they are ever born?

Since a few days before Thanksgiving, we have already been reminded that we have entered the festive season of the year and are being told that it is indeed the season to be jolly.

- But, is this indeed the season to eat, drink, and be merry?
- Should the week before Thanksgiving to the first week of the New Year be viewed as our national, joyous winter festival filled with overeating and overspending?
- Is this the time to be mindful of the bounty of the crops we have harvested and to celebrate our bounty on Black Friday by participating in the ritual of consumer spending?

- Is this the season in which we are to allow ourselves to believe that our genuine love and affection for our family and loved ones can only be shown by the amount of money we spend on Christmas gifts and presents?
- Is this the season wherein we allow our genuine affections for our loved ones to be connected to our wallets and purses?

WHAT IS A SERMON IN AFRICAN AMERICAN CHURCHES OF CHRIST?

Reflections from "Christmas According to Matthew"

Hubert G. Locke

A sermon is a discourse during Christian services of worship that is expected to fulfill multiple functions. Using the Scriptures as its source, it should inform, instruct, inspire, convict, persuade, motivate, and, if necessary, chastise its hearers. Because of its intrinsic power it should, above all else, bring about a change in the lives of those who heed its message. Few sermons accomplish all of these manifold tasks. Over the centuries, in fact, various Christian traditions have become renowned (or infamous, as the case may be) for their emphasis on—or mastery of—one or more of these homiletic purposes.

Taking note of the fact that there can be a negative dimension in preaching—as well as its positive purposes—is, at the outset, to pay tribute to Jerry Taylor's sermonic prowess. In an age of televangelists and preachers of a so-called gospel of prosperity—whose distortion of the biblical message is scandalous—one cannot help but sense the underlying integrity of Dr. Taylor's message. He remains, in every moment, faithful to the text—the sine qua non of authentic preaching! He does not use Scripture as a prop for a preconceived proclamation. Scripture, instead, is the foundation of his message and wrestling with its mysteries and meaning is a task from which he clearly does not shirk.

Jerry Taylor comes to the pulpit and its ministry from the African American wing of the Churches of Christ, where preaching has, over almost a century, taken on a life of its own. The sermon, in Black Churches of Christ, has one, overriding—almost exclusive—purpose.

It is designed, scripted, and delivered to convert sinners to Christ, to save the lost, and to redeem the fallen—only, in a cluster of churches that see themselves as the only authentic example of Christian life and worship, converting sinners and saving the lost essentially means convincing members of other Christian bodies to realize the error of their ways and to forsake denominationalism (understood as every church that isn't a Church of Christ) for membership in the true church.

As this tradition has become firmly rooted in African American Churches of Christ, it has become difficult, if not impossible, to distinguish the sermon delivered in gospel meetings—the principal evangelistic effort of Black congregations—from that heard at Sunday morning services of worship. The former—the gospel meeting message—at least has as its aim saving the lost, even if the lost are members of every other church in town. However, a gospel meeting sermon at eleven o'clock on Sunday morning, when ninety-five percent of the congregants are already faithful Church of Christ members, means that the spiritual needs of the overwhelming number of hearers go un- or severely undernourished. It has produced a collection of churches and a tradition that is well-rehearsed in first principles but whose members are sadly ill-equipped to grow, in Paul's words, to "the measure of the stature of the fullness of Christ."

The temptation to reflect on what this tradition has meant for the life and work of Black Churches of Christ is almost irresistible, but to do so would distract from the primary task at hand. We have, in Jerry Taylor's "Christmas According to Matthew," a fine example of expository preaching—a sermon whose essential purpose is to interpret a biblical text or series of biblical passages and apply their pronouncements to the life circumstances of the hearers.

Expository preaching stands at the core of the homiletic tradition in Churches of Christ and equally so in the larger Christian tradition. By its very claim—that it explains or expands on a passage of Scripture, providing an authentic interpretation of that passage's meaning and message—expository preaching presents an immense challenge. It also presents an enormous peril.

The religious tradition in Churches of Christ is built on the conviction that the Bible is the Word of God, that its writers were divinely inspired to pen the narratives, historical accounts, letters, and other writings that form the content of Scripture, and that it is this divine authorization that makes Scripture the only source of authentic faith and practice. The belief that the Bible is divinely inspired, however, does not extend to those who preach from it. No matter how much the preacher struggles with a text or passage, regardless of the depth of one's desire to be faithful in the explication of the Word, the words of the preacher are the attempt of a mere mortal to convey divine truths. It is why Paul reminds us: "we have this treasure in earthen vessels..." (2 Cor. 4:7).

One can, for this reason, especially appreciate the obvious humility with which Taylor has gone about his homiletic task. The Gospel of John records that Jesus' last words to Peter, before his ascension, were "Feed my sheep" and that he repeated these three words three times. There is a continual hunger among God's children for spiritual nourishment—to be fed with the rich substance that is to be found in the Scriptures and that guides, strengthens, and renews us for the tasks of daily living. Expository preaching, if it does not take up this broader and deeper challenge, fails to respond to one of the urgent needs of those who come, Sunday after Sunday, to hear what the Word of God has to say to them. It also fails to heed Christ's own admonition. I am grateful to find in the work of Jerry Taylor food for the hungry, especially in the season we least sense our personal and communal needs.

6

Being Still in God's Movement

Compositional Notes

This message was delivered on February 23, 2004 at the Abilene Christian University Lectureship in Abilene, Texas.

I developed this sermon from the Isaiah text under the heavy influence of several major historic events that had recently unfolded in this country. On the day I delivered this message the United States was only two years beyond the tragic event of 9/11. The war in Iraq was approaching the one year mark. America was feeling a great sense of fear. As a nation we were at ground zero. Americans desperately hungered to feel safe again. Our lives had been changed forever. In our text Isaiah describes Israel's state of emergency, which sounds like a description of a post 9/11 America. In light of this similarity, I sought to build the sermon around the big question that Isaiah raises for Israel in the text. Who can we turn to and rely upon with total confidence during a time of a national distress?

In Isaiah 40:19-24 the prophet thinks it is laughable that Israel would trust—as credible sources of national security—idol gods, international empires, and political rulers. I linger over this section of the text in order to show the clear connection between a nation's fear and the lucrative profits made by those who promise to preserve a nation's security. During this time of crisis in America several prominent Christian leaders encouraged the nation to trust in the president and the United States military. Those who spoke out against the idolatrous worship of America's president and military were accused of being unpatriotic. I felt strongly that it was imperative that I use this text to remind the audience that God, and not the United States, is the sole preserver and protector of the Christian faith.

The Isaiah text enabled me to challenge my audience to remember that in a world riveted by terrorism God serves as the only true source of security. Thus, I spent some time with Isaiah 40:31 in order to emphasize the necessity of waiting upon God to be the first respondent in addressing a national tragedy. I challenge my audience to remain still in the divine action God takes to build a world according to his brilliant vision.

BEING STILL IN GOD'S MOVEMENT

". . . those who hope in the LORD will renew their strength.
They will soar on wings like eagles; they will run and not grow weary,
they will walk and not be faint."

Isaiah 40:31

In Isaiah 40:12-31 Israel is humiliated and broken. Babylon has mercilessly shattered Israel's national spirit. A million pieces of hope are loosely scattered as ashes upon the grave of Israel's unfulfilled potential. Jerusalem has been laid waste. The temple has been pillaged and burned. The king and many high officials have been executed. Survivors, including many of the former leaders of the nation, have been deported to Babylon. Israel's theological nervous system has suffered a breakdown. Israel's entire society is at ground zero.

In light of this devastating historical situation, Israel doubts its ability to recover. Israel's frightened heart is like a haunted house filled with loud screams of fear. Toxic paranoia infectiously spreads throughout the country at pandemic proportions. The prophet knows that Israel's unresolved insecurities can cause the nation to seek security from wrong sources.

We have witnessed over the past decade how fear-driven Americans have sacrificed truth, liberty, and freedom to the idol god of security. Martin Luther once called security "the ultimate idol." Americans have put trust in the Patriot Act as if it were a divine edict issued from God's throne. The state of the church in America is similar to that of Israel in Babylonian captivity. Like Babylon, capitalistic greed has established unparalleled mastery over the American church. The house of prayer for all nations has been taken captive by monetary thieves and turned into a disguised den of religious robbers (Mark 11:17). Capitalistic greed discourages the church from speaking prophetic truth to the cunning and craftiness of men in their deceitful scheming (Eph. 4:14).

Major prophetic voices in America have been silenced by well disguised assassinations. The Christian media also joined the opposition movement to silence the prophets. The church's prophetic voices have been relegated to a state of obscurity. Christian media unapologetically gives prime time to voices that sanction America's consumerism by using such slogans as "name it and claim it."

Nevertheless, the church needs the voice of prophets. Like Israel, the church needs prophets that do not speak of a distant future or romanticize about a nostalgic past. Like Israel, the church needs prophets that courageously speak truth in the midst of a national environment that tolerates lies and falsehoods.

Prophetic voices are needed because televangelists sell religion as a drug to the masses. Religious drug dealers use televised programs to turn their viewers into religious addicts. Christian theatrical stagecraft fails to critique the unjust societal structures in America. Isaiah is an example of courageous prophetic leadership that confronts religious corruption.

Isaiah begins his discourse by exposing the futility of idol gods. He compares the all-encompassing hand of the living God to the lifeless and impotent hands of idols. He asks, "Who has measured the waters in the hollow of his hand. With the breadth of his hand he marked off the heavens. Who has held the dust of the earth in a basket, or has weighed the mountains on the scales and the hills in a balance" (40:12).

Isaiah says, "A craftsman casts it and a goldsmith overlays it with gold and fashions silver chains for it. A man too poor to present such an offering selects wood that will not rot" (40:19-20). God dresses the earth in all its splendor and glory, but idol gods cannot even dress themselves. Isaiah uses biting humor when he says that the idol god of a poor man is left naked of gold and silver. In this statement, Isaiah sets into motion a relevant set of questions. How can idol gods secure Israel when idol gods have to be secured by humans? Why should Israel hope in idol gods when their very existence depends upon the work of craftsmen?

Isaiah's craftsmen are similar to the craftsmen of every period in history. Craftsmen of idol gods make their greatest financial profits during a climate of fear. Politicians have learned that it is advantageous to promise an increase in national security. Many crafty politicians have crafted their careers on the toxic landscape of American fear. They promise to secure Americans from crime, drugs, terrorism, socialism, communism, immigration, and economic depressions.

The church in America is not exempt from the politics of fear. During major political elections the American church is often highjacked. It is turned into an aggressive political machine that helps create a climate of fear and helps get voters to the polls. In such seasons of fear it becomes easy for the church to exalt America above the kingdom of God.

During times of war, America's military is given credit as being the main preserver of Christianity around the world. An "insecure" attitude tempts the church to view America's military as if it were God's army. Might this be a reason why the church remains noticeably undisturbed as the defense budget grows bigger each year?

Halliburton announced on Friday, July 25, 2005, that its KBR division, responsible for carrying out Pentagon contracts, experienced a 284 percent increase in operating profits during the second quarter of that year. The increase in profits was primarily due to the Pentagon's payment of "award fees" for what military officials call "good" or "very good" work done by KBR in the Middle East for America's taxpayers and the troops.

The age of terrorism is proving to be very profitable for the idol god industry. Fear of terrorist attacks drives up the public demand for the manufacture of the idols of defense weapons. The size of America's defense budget can be viewed as an indication of the size of America's national "insecurity." It is not unusual for "prophets" to get in the way of the "corporate profits" of craftsmen who make defense weapons. When they do get in the way they are swiftly addressed. Peace movements that decrease fear in the public square are often seen as socialistic obstructionists to the monopolized concentration of wealth in this country. Much of the monopolized concentration of capital is found in the defense industry.

On American currency there is the inscription "In God We Trust." Which "god" does the inscription refer to? Is America's trust in the God of Abraham, Isaac, and Jacob or is it in the idol gods of economic power and military might? As we reflect upon the meaning of this inscription, the church does well to remember Isaiah's first major point of his discourse in Isaiah 40:12-31. He tells Israel not to trust in idol gods as the source of any positive benefit to God's people.

Isaiah moves now to discourage Israel from putting trust in the power of nations.

Isaiah compares the power of international empires with the eternal greatness of God in Isaiah 40:15-17: "Surely the nations are like a drop in a bucket; they are regarded as dust on the scales; he weighs the islands as though they were fine dust. Lebanon is not sufficient for altar fires, nor its animals enough for burnt offerings. Before him all the nations are as nothing; they are regarded by him as worthless and less than nothing."

Babylon stands far above other nations of the earth economically, militarily, and politically. But Isaiah wants Israel to know that despite Babylon's international reputation Babylon is not invincible. Yes, the church sincerely prays for the welfare of America and all the nations of the earth. However, when the American church pledges allegiance to the flag of the United States of America and to the republic for which it stands, it does so with the understanding that its ultimate allegiance is uncompromisingly reserved for God.

Despite how insecure the church feels in the world, the United States of America, as a nation, is not the ultimate protector and defender of the Christian faith. The church does not place its trust in national security, social security, or homeland security. The church in every generation must boldly declare under the threat of persecution, scorn, and retaliation that its highest allegiance is to a kingdom that is not of this world.

Many in the American church believe that the biggest threat to Christianity today is Islam. Some believe that drastic measures must be taken to arrest Islam's expansive growth in America and around the world. Such urgency has caused the church to bypass a time of actively waiting inside of God's movement. Instead, the church looks to the federal government to take decisive actions to protect Christianity against the rising Muslim influence. It also expects the government to protect it against any possible persecution that might come at the hands of Muslims. However, Isaiah would make the case that it is not any nation's job to protect God's people from persecution.

If the church in America is not being persecuted, we must ask the church to respond to some tough questions. What has the church exchanged for America's protective custody of Christianity? What has the church agreed to overlook? Has the church agreed to look the other way while American chemical companies use northern Mexico as a dump site for their toxic waste? Have Christian leaders agreed to ignore the increased Klan mentality of white supremacy and racial separation that seem to have found a comfortable home in many of their congregations today? Has the church agreed to ignore the fact that America has gotten drunk on the wine of wealth and that it staggers in the pride of its status of being the world's sole superpower?

The only way the church can escape suffering is to compromise with the kingdoms of this world.

In the book of Revelation John calls for opposition to any attempt to compromise with the Babylonian Superpower. John encourages the church to remain defiant in the face of imperial power. The church must not lift up her soul in worship of the empire. The church has survived through the ages not because it depended upon nations and empires, but because it relied upon the strength of Almighty God.

Isaiah the prophet says that Yahweh is superior to everything on the earth, "Have you not understood since the earth was founded? He sits enthroned above the circle of the earth, and its people are like grasshoppers. He stretches out the heavens like a canopy, and spreads them out like a tent to live in" (40:21-22). Yahweh is the only supra-power.

After discounting the power of idol gods and nations, Isaiah moves next to focus attention upon the powerlessness of princes and rulers. Isaiah tells Israel that if idols and nations cannot rescue a domesticated people, neither can rulers and princes. Isaiah says: "He brings princes to naught and reduces the rulers of this world to nothing. No sooner are they planted, no sooner are they sown, no sooner do they take root in the ground, than he blows on them and they wither, and a whirlwind sweeps them away like chaff" (40:23-24).

Evangelicals played a significant role in electing George W. Bush twice as president of the United States. Many churches endorsed Mr. Bush as a "Christian candidate." Conservative Evangelicals made it no secret that they expected Mr. Bush to use the oval office to influence the United States government to advance Christianity throughout American society and the world. Their expectations were similar to the expectations of the framers of the Westminster Confession.

Framers of the Westminster Confession clearly envisioned a role for Christian teachings in the affairs of the state. Thus they claimed that "the job of a civil magistrate is to protect the Church and to ensure that all the ordinances of God are observed."

The pilgrims who sailed to America on the Mayflower in 1620 believed that the new colony they were founding would "advance . . . the Christian religion" (as stated in the Mayflower Compact).

It would be wise for the church in America to refrain from endorsing any person as "God's candidate." When the church endorses a person as "God's candidate," the entire Christian community is normally judged on the grounds of that candidate's conduct. Just because a politician says he or she is a born-again Christian does not warrant the Christian community surrendering its agenda to that person's political aspirations.

After Isaiah expresses conviction about the futility of trusting in idols, nations, and rulers, he focuses attention upon God who is more than able to deliver. The prophet compares and contrasts these inferior sources to Yahweh's superior might. In 40:25, Isaiah asks Israel "to whom will you compare God? Who in all creation is equal to God?" In verse 26 the prophet says, "Lift up your eyes and look to the heavens; who created all these? He brings out the starry hosts, one by one, and calls them each by name. Because of his great power and mighty strength, not one of them is missing."

Isaiah instructs Israel to look up and catch a glimpse of what is above and beyond the limiting exile. Israel must synchronize its eyes with God's eyes. Focusing only upon a bleak picture of exile is what causes Israel to grow weary and tired. Israel is blessed in that God empowers his people to see beyond the twisted face of an ugly historical reality.

Today it is through God's divine paradigm that the church envisions a beautiful world beyond the wreckage of the present world. The church stubbornly believes that God will eventually actualize his vision of beauty in this world torn by tragedy. The kingdom vision is bigger than any group, any race, any political party, or any nation.

However, the church understands that unless God implements the kingdom vision, the people of the earth will perish.

- Without this vision, the world is blind and hopeless.
- Without this vision, the clash of civilizations will reach new heights.
- Without this vision, children in America's public school system are given recess on the toxic playground of an inferior education.
- Without this vision, the public school system sends miseducated children into toxic inner city environments to become playmates with gang members and drug dealers.
- Without this vision, the church applauds America as it spends more money on building new prisons than it does on rebuilding a broken public school system.
- Without this vision, religious hatred leads the human family into a new era of balkanization.
- Without this vision, the church has little voice to prevent America from slowly staggering into the theater of war between the racial and ethnic groups in this country.

Though the church hungers to see the righteous kingdom vision become a reality in the context of exile, it still must wait on God. The implementation of the kingdom vision depends upon God's inspiration and not human initiation. When the church waits upon God, it then exists within the divine rhythm of God's activity. When the church waits upon God it reflects an understanding that:

- God is a God of both stillness and movement.
- God is a God of both waiting and working.
- God is a God of both solitude and service.
- God is a God of both prayer and practice.

Before the church moves it must become still. As the church waits it engages in active and attentive listening to God's directives. The church must see God as the traffic director of life. God does not want the church to rush through the dangerous intersections and crossroads of life without respecting God's authoritative direction.

One weekend, in a rush to enjoy Christian fellowship, I approached an intersection. I looked both ways and, after observing no approaching traffic, I proceeded to cross the intersection, only to be met by the energetic protest of my fellow passengers. They brought it to my attention that I was in fact running through a traffic light that was definitely red. I was horrified by the fact that I had violated the law due to an honest failure to pay attention to the traffic light. The fact that I was on my way to participate in a Christian activity did not excuse my action.

I had committed what law enforcement calls a "moving violation." My movement through the intersection was without lawful permission. My action failed to acknowledge the existence and purpose of the traffic light. How often does the church commit moving violations in its attempt to realize the great kingdom vision? How often does rushing to complete programs and projects in the name of God cause the church to move through the intersections of ministry without respect for God's divine timing?

Isaiah tells Israel to wait on God.

- When the church waits on God, it is able see that God's wisdom is superior to wit, reason, or human intelligence.
- When the church waits on God, it behaves as a good waiter or waitress, respectfully taking God's orders into the kitchen of life and returning to his table with an entrée according to his specifications.
- When the church waits on God, it is not controlled by watches, planners, and schedules, but by the calendar of eternity.
- When the church waits on God, it gives up its dependence on military might to advance the Christian cause around the world.
- When the church waits on God, it will boldly declare that bombs and politics will never establish a lasting peace in the world.
- When the church waits on God, the church will also declare that only the Prince of Peace can produce peace on earth as each heart is conquered with the loving reign of God.
- When the church waits on God, it gives up its need to be financially backed by wealthy capitalists who see money as the only god that really makes things happen in the world.
- When the church waits on God, it learns to live in the eternity of now.

When the church waits upon the Lord, it expresses its true nature of being a waiting community as described in Luke 24:49. Jesus commands the founding members of the church to wait in Jerusalem until they have been clothed with power from on high. Jesus does not tell the church to wait on the power of the oval office. Jesus does not tell the church to wait on the power of the Senate. Jesus does not tell the church to wait on the power of the U.S. House of Representatives. Jesus tells the church to wait on the power of the Holy Spirit.

While Isaiah emphasizes Israel's need to wait, he also stresses the point that God is a God of movement. Waiting upon the Lord does not imply that the church resigns from its commitment to seeking justice. Waiting upon the Lord means that the church has learned to wait by practicing prayerful active listening until God gives the green light. Once God gives the green light of direction, he expects the church to move. He does not want the church to sit still blocking the intersection of progress.

Isaiah says, "those who hope in the LORD will renew their strength."

They will soar on wings like eagles. *That's movement.*
They will run and not grow weary. *That's movement.*
They will walk and not be faint. *That's movement.*

- When God moves, Nebuchadnezzar's image collapses and fiery furnaces open up with God's liberated church marching in step with the Son of Man.
- When God moves, Goliath greed on Wall Street is hit in the head with the rock of courageous truth from the sling shot of economic justice.
- When God moves, Jericho's walls of racial profiling "come a tumbling down" and the sun of prophetic truth stands still until racial and gender equality in America becomes an undisputed reality.
- When God moves, foundations of the Birmingham jail are shaken and political prisoners are set free to baptize their captors in the river of compassion.
- When God moves, fear mongering politicians can no longer cause the church any alarm, because the church has not been given a spirit of fear, but a spirit of love, courage, and soundness of mind.

Trying to prevent God's movement in the world is like trying to prevent the breaking of an incoming wave. Trying to prevent God's movement in the world is like trying to restrain the weather by throwing a lasso around the neck of a tornado.

Ask Saul, who sought without success to stop the newly formed Christian movement by kicking against the pricks. Ask the Roman emperors, who fed Christians to the lions, crucified them upside down, and burned their bodies.

- Though the church seems tired;
- though the church seems weary;
- though the church seems worn;
- though the church's energy seems depleted, the church will wait upon the Lord.
- God puts walking in the church's tired feet.
- God puts flapping in the church's weakened wings.
- God puts running in the church's lame legs.

The church has hit the "refresh button" by waiting upon the Lord. Through its refreshed strength the church rises from the ruins of exile in Babylon. The church has the renewed stamina to march against the nation's underlying commitment to white supremacy. The church has the Spirit-filled activism to expose an imbalanced capitalism that socializes economic loss and privatizes economic profits.

As a result of the church spending time in the holding pattern of intentional waiting, it has received its "marching orders." The church has "marching orders" to speak in agreement with that which is righteous in America. May his truth keep marching on!

PROPHETIC PREACHING IN THE TRADITION OF JOHN THE BAPTIST:

A Response to "Being Still in God's Movement"

Frank A. Thomas

Recently, there has been a tremendous amount of discussion in homiletical and theological circles as to the true nature and contemporary relevance of "prophetic preaching." Particularly in the African American community, there has arisen a conversation among preachers as to whether or not, given the fact that we are in the post-civil rights era, and the fact that some African Americans have risen in wealth and power, if there is still a need to be "prophetic." First, we must acknowledge that there are many models defining what it means to be prophetic, and it would probably help discussion if we would clarify what we mean when we say "prophetic" and delineate a model of what we mean when we say "prophetic preaching." The term "prophetic preaching" can be used glibly and in broad brush strokes, and it's helpful to define the terms.

One of the best models for prophetic preaching is that of John the Baptist in the New Testament. John the Baptist had total allegiance to God's domain and refused to endorse any theological or political ideology as identical with God's eternal rule. John demanded of all people allegiance to God's universal and sovereign domain. Allegiance to this domain forced John to radically challenge the religious and social system of his time by establishing his ministry in the wilderness, where he preached and baptized for the remission of sin. Up until that time, the priests at the temple were the ones to baptize and forgive sin, but John proclaimed a new spiritual order that questioned the legitimacy of the Temple order and gave him the authority, once held by the Temple, to baptize and forgive sin. John's message calls into question the legitimacy of the entire Temple religious order of Jesus' day. John also challenged Herod's behavior in marrying his brother's wife and was put in prison because of his proclamation. John equally challenged the behavior of the ruling and wealthy class. John was subsequently beheaded for his prophetic declaration because of his allegiance to God's sovereign reign and rule.

John provides a clear standard for prophetic preaching: the sermon based upon an allegiance to God's domain, a new spiritual order, calls into question the present religious and political system, even challenging the ruling class.

Jerry Taylor, in this sermon, stands in the prophetic tradition of John the Baptist and presents an excellent model of contemporary prophetic preaching. The sermon demonstrates an allegiance to God's sovereign rule and reign, and based in that allegiance, challenges the present-day religious and political order. He starts with the church (the Temple) and its comfortable and easy collusion with America. Taylor believes that "the state of the church in America is similar to that of Israel in Babylonian captivity," and that fear has allowed capitalistic greed to establish "unparalleled mastery over the American church." Taylor questions the uncritical stance of American churches towards America's greed and unregulated capitalistic mammon. Taylor assails the church's collusion with the American military, American politics, and America's corporate profits. As an example of the specificity of Taylor's critique, he says:

> Has the church agreed to look the other way while American chemical companies use northern Mexico as a dump site for their toxic waste? Have Christian leaders agreed to ignore the increased Klan mentality of white supremacy and racial separation that seem to have found a comfortable home in many of their congregations today? Has the church agreed to ignore the

fact that America has gotten drunk on the wine of wealth and that it staggers in the pride of its status of being the world's sole super power?

Taylor calls the American church into question when he suggests that when the church knowingly "pledges allegiance to the flag of the United States of America and to the republic for which it stands, it does so with the understanding that its ultimate allegiance is uncompromisingly reserved for God." The church is giving ultimate allegiance to someone or something other than God. In stark contrast, Taylor is like John the Baptist, a voice crying out in the wilderness.

Based upon his clear vision of God's kingdom, Taylor challenges the hearer not to trust in the security of the world (America), but to trust in God's sovereign reign and rule over the world. Based upon the reality of terrorism, fear is running rampant in our time. Fear becomes an idol and fear is used to justify many injustices and because the church is afraid, the church goes along. Believers, just like the Israelites in the Isaiah text, are to trust in God's security and wait upon the Lord. As Taylor says, "the implementation of the kingdom vision depends upon God's inspiration and not human initiation. When the church waits upon God, it then exists within the divine rhythm of God's activity." God is a God of movement and the church is to trust God and wait rather than make alliances based upon the needs of fear-based security.

Despite the movement of many African Americans into the middle-class values of America, there is still a critical need for prophetic preaching. The sovereign reign and rule of God is the ultimate allegiance and that allegiance critiques middle-class American values regardless of the race or class of the proponent of those values.

7

The Ventriloquist

Compositional Notes

I delivered this sermon on February 21, 2003, as a part of the Fab Five Revival, an annual event held at the Light of the World Church of Christ in Dallas, Texas. The audience consists mainly of African American members of Churches of Christ from around the city of Dallas.

My intention at the very beginning of the sermon is to help the audience pay attention to how those with external power viewed human life in the first century. The life of a slave is only valued for the amount of money he or she is able to bring to the slave owners. In Acts 16:16, Luke says that the slave girl earned a great deal of money for her owners by fortune-telling. This verse also shows that as a result of Paul and Silas being men of prayer they are empowered not only to engage the slave girl on their way to the "place of prayer," but they actually liberate her from corrupt internal and external powers.

I use the imagery of a python to subtly make the point that once again a snake spirit infiltrates the life of a woman and uses her as a mouthpiece to speak on behalf of a well-hidden power. At this stage in the sermon, I point out the relationship ventriloquists have with the dummies they use in their performances. Their relationship is no different from the relationship that exists between the slave girl and the internal spirit that dominates her. Neither is their relationship any different than the one that exists between political front men and the corporate and economic powers that pull their strings.

In Acts 16:19-24, Luke makes it clear that there are consequences when servants of God use their spiritual power to set slave girls free from economic exploitation. The venomous python spirit strikes back when slave owners' financial profits are threatened. At this point in the sermon I stress the importance of being willing to suffer for the sake of prayerfully healing those caught in the greedy grips of economic exploitation. God stands ready to deliver. A gospel that is insensitive to the economic injustice that exploits the poor is a perverted gospel!

THE VENTRILOQUIST

Acts 16:16-34

The message I will share with you tonight is entitled "The Ventriloquist" and is extracted from the text of Acts 16:16-34. My intention is to lead our thinking in the examination of the nature of real power versus the nature of artificial power. We will see the superiority of internal power against the inferiority of external force. The text reveals how external power is manipulated, misused, and abused. External power depends on the exterior symbols of authority such as tin badges, special dress, uniforms, weapons, capital, positions, and prestige. People are moved by these external symbols of power, but God is not impressed. Man looks at the outward appearance, but God looks at the heart.

Paul, Silas, and their companions had learned the superiority of the internal power given by God. They were connected to the real superpower. The text reveals that Paul and Silas were men of prayer and says they were on their way to the place of prayer.

- Prayer brings renewal, restoration, and revival.
- Prayer transports us into that secret place of peace that is secure from all alarms.
- Prayer is that place where spirit touches Spirit, and where God touches our internal being.
- Prayer equips us to redeem any negative situation that life shoves in our face.
- Prayer empowers us to set the captives free.
- Prayer tenderizes our hearts and enables us to liberate our oppressors from their greedy appetite for external control.
- Prayer arranges our hearts to even love those who beat and flog us publicly with the mean-spirited rods of misrepresentations and the stinging whips of false accusations.
- Prayer maintains the health and strength of our voices that cry out with crystal clarity from the darkest place of a hellish dungeon where power-crazed men thirsty for external domination have imprisoned us.
- Prayer teaches us that, though external liberty can be withheld, freedom is an intrinsic quality that cannot be

denied nor destroyed. Liberty is exercised outwardly, but freedom is an internal attitude of the heart untouchable by the hands and actions of men.

Our text exposes the fact that, though Paul and Silas were men of prayer, they were beaten and flogged publicly because they had set a slave girl free from a spirit of divination. The slave girl had a spirit of divination, a "spirit of Python." A spirit of Python is an allusion to Pythian Apollo, the god who was supposed to be embodied in a snake at Delphi. The snake-god at Delphi allegedly supplied the priestess with oracles. According to Plutarch, the "Python men" were ventriloquists. The slave girl at Philippi had been trained by her owners to give oracular utterances by means of ventriloquism. They used her in this manner for financial gain.

We have Python men and women today who worship the snake-god. When Python men and women speak, they speak with a forked tongue; whatever comes out of their mouths cannot be trusted, and it is impossible to know who is speaking. They move and open their mouths, but they are not in control of their own voices. Python men and women speak, but they do not choose their own words. Python speech is moving and effective but is under the charming influence of the spirit of the Python snake-god.

There are many people who are well trained but are just like this slave girl. They have been taught by their owners to give oracular utterances by means of ventriloquism. When they speak, it is impossible to see the invisible hand going up their backs that controls the movement of their mouths. It is hard to identify the person or the power that serves as the ventriloquist. The ventriloquist always stays behind the scenes and makes it appear that the dummy is doing the speaking and the acting.

- The dummy does not have a mind, therefore he does not think for himself.

- Though the dummy looks human, it has no humanity.
- Though the dummy has eyes, it cannot see the blatant display of injustice occurring right in front of his face.
- Though the dummy has ears, it cannot hear the cries and woes of the oppressed that scream for liberation from their miserable conditions.
- Though the dummy has a head, it has no memory of the sacred lives of past generations who laid down their lives so things could be better in this day.
- The dummy has hands and limbs, but it is powerless to do anything that would relieve the heavy burden of economic exploitation experienced by the poor living in the inner cities of America.
- The dummy is manipulated and controlled by the ventriloquist.

Paul confronted the spirit of the Python god that was using this girl as a ventriloquist uses a dummy. Paul exorcised this Python spirit in the name of Jesus Christ. Once the snake-god's spirit had been driven out of this slave girl, she regained her sanity. The masters of this slave girl were furious because this deed threatened them financially. The owners thought that this single act of healing would disrupt the economy of the city of Philippi. The owners' held the conviction that their economic prosperity could only be maintained by the sick condition of this slave girl; their luxury and comfort depended upon maintaining the misery and ruin of another human being.

Paul simply addressed the spirit that had invaded the personhood of the slave girl. The text reveals that the owners were in fellowship with this spirit of Python because it enabled them to receive great financial gain. The owners worked in cooperation with the Python spirit to financially exploit the superstitious ignorance of the masses. Therefore, when Paul drove out the Python spirit, he was actually attacking the spirit of an unjust economic system. Paul refused to compromise with this spirit of the snake-god.

If Paul had been vain and full of ego, he could have been seduced by the flattering words spoken by this slave girl. She kept following Paul and Silas while constantly repeating positive words about them such as "these men are servants of the Most High God, who are telling you the way to be saved." Paul could have used the spirit of Python in this slave girl to promote his work in Philippi. He could have joined in with the owners in exploiting her and made a deal with the owners to employ the girl as a good marketing tool for his ministry. Yet, Paul was not deceived by the positive affirmations. Paul also understood that God does not have fellowship with demons nor accepts their testimony as praise!

By driving out the Python spirit from the girl, Paul sent a clear message to the owners and the spirit of the economic system that he flatly rejected the offer of partnership. When Paul demonstrated his willingness to challenge the spirit of the economic system, the spiritual powers of wickedness sought to destroy him. Attacking the spirit of any organization or institution will get you killed! It was not until Jesus confronted the spirit of economic injustice in the Jerusalem Temple in Mark 11 that the leaders of the Temple conspired together how they might kill him. Slaves in the South brought great wealth to many people and it was the presidential decision to emancipate the slaves that caused Republican President Abraham Lincoln to be shot by an assassin. Finally, it was the call for this nation to redistribute wealth that caused Dr. King to lose his life on a balcony in Memphis.

It does not matter what religious or political party you are with; you will be killed if you go up against the spirit of that system. You will be permitted to survive within an organization as long as you give the impression that you are in partnership with the spirit of that group. You may break every moral law of that organization and still be protected by the organization because your allegiance is to the spirit of that system. However, if you confront the spirit of an organization, that system will destroy you immediately, regardless of how many of its moral rules you keep.

The owners, out of bitterness and revenge, used everything at their disposal to destroy Paul and Silas. They turned the city officials against them, and they even used the prejudice of an unthinking mob to join in the hateful attack on Paul and Silas. People who hate you for interfering with their economic exploitation will use every system within their reach as weapons to destroy your life.

Our nation has become intoxicated with her status as the world's only superpower. America, with its unmatched nuclear arsenal, is the nation that possesses the greatest capacity to destroy human life. Our beloved country must be careful that we not become like Germany in the previous century, where one madman led an entire nation into a killing spree and whose hands to this day are dripping with the innocent blood of the Jewish people.

There is something evil and atrocious being covertly implemented in our nation and in our world tonight. It seems that we, as world citizens, are riding on an international bus that has been hijacked by a small group of power elite whose minds have been baptized into the concept of aggressive externalized force. As citizens, we are being driven against our will across a bridge sabotaged with the explosives of hatred, violence, and mass destruction. Many on this bus are fearful to speak or act lest they be accused of being unpatriotic terrorist sympathizers. This is not the hour wherein we can allow fear and selfish interests to silence our voices. We must not blind ourselves to the fixings that are going on in our world tonight. We cannot afford to develop paralysis in our Christian activism on this important issue.

"THE VENTRILOQUIST"

An Evangelical Reflection

David Faust

When I listen to a sermon (or prepare to deliver one myself) I keep certain assumptions in mind.

1. *Good preaching is Bible-based.* Our twenty-first century world resembles ancient Israel where there was "a famine of hearing the words of the Lord" (Amos 8:11). "All Scripture is God-breathed" and divinely designed for positive uses like "teaching" and "training in righteousness," and for negative uses like "rebuking" and "correcting" (2 Timothy 3:16).
2. *Good preaching is Christ-centered.* The Apostle Paul said, "We do not preach ourselves, but Jesus Christ as Lord" (2 Cor. 4:5). At the core of the gospel are the truths "of first importance" concerning the death, burial, and resurrection of Christ (1 Cor. 15:3, 4). No matter the text or topic of a sermon, somehow it must point to Christ and the cross.
3. *Good preaching builds faith, hope, and love.* Preaching is an act of love—an unselfish gift designed to meet the listener's deepest needs. The preacher's job is not to beat people down but to build them up—not mainly to philosophize, criticize, or apologize, but to evangelize, bringing good news to those who need a faith lift and an infusion of hope.
4. *Good preaching connects with the listeners and their needs.* There's nothing boring about a good sermon. It is timely,

relevant, and interesting. It engages the mind, heart, and will. It educates and motivates, comforts and convicts, prods and persuades, soothes and sharpens, combines inspiration with perspiration, faith with works. Since the goal is to blend biblical truth with human need, the preacher must know the people, know the culture, know the Scriptures, and link all of them together in a compelling way.

Jerry Taylor is an effective communicator who finds unique insights in a biblical text and relays them to his listeners in a compelling way. Let's evaluate his sermon, "The Ventriloquist," by applying the four criteria mentioned above.

Is it biblical? The sermon finds its roots in Acts 16. It highlights the great biblical themes of prayer, faith, courage, and priorities based on the kingdom of God. In developing the biblical text, I would like to see Brother Taylor offer a more detailed explanation of "the spirit of Python." The Python spirit is suggested by the Greek text and by biblical commentators, but it needs more explanation by the preacher since English translations do not explicitly mention it. And how do we know that the slave girl's owners trained her "to give oracular utterances by means of ventriloquism"? Since this isn't stated in the biblical text, what evidence suggests it? Was ventriloquism common in the ancient world? (This may seem a minor detail, but since the sermon's title and theme depend on it, more explanation of the ventriloquism concept would strengthen the message.)

Is the sermon Christ-centered? Yes, but the message could give more prominence to the cross. The sermon's stated goal is to contrast "real power" with "artificial power," for the real "superpower" is Christ who possesses all authority in heaven and earth (Matt. 28:18). Paul and Silas cast the demon out of the slave girl "in the name of Jesus Christ" (Acts 16:18), and later in the text, their message to the Philippian jailer was, "Believe in the Lord Jesus, and you will be saved—you and your household" (v. 31). Before the sermon ends I would like to see the preacher plainly circle back to the cross—the symbol of true power where we find courage to confront the spiritual challenges of our day. There is a natural opportunity to focus on the cross in the section of the sermon that says, "Attacking the spirit of any organization or institution will get you killed!"

Does the sermon build faith, hope, and love? Yes—and it stirs self-examination with its prophetic challenge to critique our culture. Brother Taylor points out that by freeing the slave girl and refusing any collusion with her owners, Paul was "attacking the spirit of an unjust economic system" that used and abused a human being for financial gain. There is hope in this story for anyone who suffers the pain of injustice, and the sermon rightly calls us to put our faith in the Lord rather than in human institutions.

Does the sermon connect with the listeners and their needs? Perhaps. Toward the end of the sermon Brother Taylor focuses on America's "intoxication with her status as the world's only superpower." While one role of a prophetic message is to disturb the comfortable, I would like to see the preacher offer more practical application in this section. Is the main point merely to stir outrage against our government's military policies? How should the listener put into practice the "Christian activism" that Brother Taylor advocates? Surely he wants us to do more than simply feel irritated with those who lead our nation. How can the preacher help us be doers of the Word, not hearers only (James 1:22)?

Genuine spiritual power does not reside in political strongholds but in the hearts of Christ-followers who act justly, love mercy, and walk humbly with God (Micah 6:8). In Acts 16, we see this divine power not only in a slave girl liberated from abuse, but also in the home of the Philippian jailer whose family came to faith in Christ, and after being baptized they were "filled with joy, because they had come to believe in God" (v. 34). The gospel of Christ made everything new. Then and now, that's where the real power and joy are found.

8

Courageous Compassion

Compositional Notes

In 2007 I presented this message in chapel services on the campuses of Abilene Christian University, Ozark Christian College, and Pepperdine University.

The sermon begins with the opening scene of the demoniac living in the cemetery. I start with this scene because I think it is essential to helping the audience see the absurdity in allowing a human being to exist in such an environment. The cemetery has a horrible stigma. It is a location of impurity. Death is its trademark. It is a context of cold isolation absent of the warmth of communal relationships.

My intention is to solidly establish sympathy for the demoniac. There is a problem if the listener cannot feel any sympathy for this helpless man. Any listener who is untouched by this story is unlikely to be moved by similar suffering unfolding in their own community. Jesus' heroic actions in the text allow me to use him as the eloquent model of courageous compassion. Jesus is not repelled by the impure state of the man's living condition. Instead, Jesus places himself at risk in order to rescue a human being from self annihilation. In Jesus, compassion overrides fear and love wins the day. On the heels of raising Jesus as the model for courageous compassion the sermon summons the listener to do the same.

Since the university chapel audiences consist mainly of eighteen to twenty-two year olds, I thought it necessary to use language with which they can best identify. I point out that Legion still shows up in the form of those who cut themselves with the stones of drugs, alcohol, wild parties, and sexual immorality. I want the audience to see that Legion is like the student who refuses to practice self discipline. Legion is like some young men and women who exhaust the patience and resources of their communities. People who once were connected to them have cut ties.

This sermon sums up the challenge issued in each message of this book. The book title calls for Christians to continue displaying a courageous compassion in a world bent on self destruction. The heart of Jesus will not allow Christians to abandon humanity even though humanity chooses to live in the cemetery as a normal way of life.

COURAGEOUS COMPASSION

Mark 5:1-20

Jesus encounters a man living in the cemetery. The cemetery is a place for the interment of the dead; it is not a place for the living. In the more primitive mind, the idea of a cemetery conjures up the scary images of evil spirits. To the modern mind, the cemetery is the prophetic mouthpiece that eloquently speaks of human mortality. There are no isolated fortresses strong enough to protect the human imagination against the forced entry of thoughts about death and dying. The cemetery reminds us of a suffering world that is living in the dark valley of the shadow of death right outside the prestigious gates to our comfort zones.

The vast majority of the global population is living in the cold context of death while it watches each day the fresh digging of its own grave. Entire groups on our planet are being destroyed through the demonic means of genocide, ethnic cleansing, starvation, diseases, and both civil and uncivil wars. Their desperate cry for help must never be seen as a disruptive intrusion into our well-arranged system of comfort and prosperity.

The need of our present hour is for a courageous compassion that refuses to recoil in the frowning face of a world that has gone mad. A courageous compassion prevents apathetic contentment with our way of life while we watch the world display its contentment with the way of death.

In a first-century mind, the cemetery is believed to be the dwelling place of demons. Therefore, in our biblical text, the man's dwelling place and bizarre actions are religiously interpreted as demon possession. The demonic spirit destroys the man's awareness of the defiled state of his living condition. He accepts living in a social context of death as a normal way of life. Since his community believes that he is demon possessed, it also accepts his dwelling in the cemetery as a normal way of life for him.

The community's religious belief permits it to view the man as less than human, and it finds justification for leaving him in his proper place among the dead because it keeps him at a safe distance away from the community. His savage and beastly behavior makes him unfit to dwell in a civilized community of law and order. He is left to a life of self-mutilation and mad ramblings through the tombs. He picks up rocks and stones and uses them as knives to cut into his own flesh. A drive through some of our modern cities will give us a picture of people who continue to pick up the rocks of crack cocaine, which they use to cut deeply into their own character and human spirit. We also catch a modern glimpse of this behavior when we visit secret parties where powdered cocaine, methamphetamine, alcohol, and ecstasy are used as rocks and stones to self-destructively cut into one's own life.

The spirit of death kills every trace of hope in this man and drives him to express irrational and bizarre behavior. No one in his community can bind, tame, or subdue him. Those who express this kind of behavior and attitude in our communities today are already pegged as prime prospects for crime, involvement in hate groups, membership in violent gangs, and eventually a lifelong internment in federal or state prison. Often our communities feel powerless to help such individuals who seem prone to violent and incorrigible behavior. Sometimes we feel overwhelmed when trying to make a meaningful difference in a world that seems so bent in the direction of hatred and violence. Like a lunatic, our world is prancing around in the cemetery of incivility, refusing to be bound, tamed, or subdued. How can we respond to the bizarre and irrational behavior of a world that has gone hatefully wild? How can the Christian community respond?

The Jewish Purity Code prevents the man's religious community from coming near him because his dwelling is in the tombs. Flat stones were placed upon the graves as markers to warn passers-by that they should avoid becoming ceremonially unclean by accidentally trespassing. The purity code is the religious system that the Jews used in first-century Palestine to distinguish between those who are pure and impure. Jesus' behavior demonstrates a courageous compassion that goes beyond the religious restrictions of a purity code. He is the embodiment and the personification of courageous compassion.

Compassion is the capacity to "feel with." In the Old Testament the word compassion has rich semantic associations. In Hebrew (as well as in Aramaic), the word usually translated as "compassion" is the plural of a noun that in its singular form means "womb." "A woman feels compassion or (natural affection) for the child of her own womb; a man feels compassion or (natural affection) for his brother, who comes from the same womb." God is the womb that gives birth to all of life, and all human beings are brothers and sisters that come from the same creative life-giving womb of God.

This understanding of compassion enables us to sincerely "feel with" our fellow human beings and to truly care about the physical and spiritual well being of our brothers and sisters who still reside in cemetery conditions in this world. Courageous compassion opens our eyes to the cemetery conditions all around us in our inner cities, suburbs, ghettoes, and plush neighborhoods. Courageous compassion does not withdraw us from the cemetery but drives us to it with the life-giving power of love that can resurrect those who are trapped in a context of death. Courageous compassion enables us to see the beautiful humanity behind the person's ugly self-destructive behavior. The courageously compassionate presence of Christ interacts with the man and emancipates him from the negative influence that dominated his entire being.

Through direct action, Jesus confronts the spirit of internal oppression. Jesus does not exercise political correctness or diplomatic peace talks in his effort to remove the tyrannical power of evil. As a result of Jesus' courageously compassionate act, the man no longer parades about as an uncontrollable lunatic. His talents, gifts, and abilities are reclaimed and rescued from being wasted by a demonic dysfunction. His personal change becomes breaking news on every major news network. His change creates such a commotion that people from miles around come out to witness the transformation.

Upon hearing the good news about the man's personal change, we are inclined to think that the community is going to wildly celebrate and express appreciation to Jesus for healing a member of their community that they themselves were powerless to help. Instead of the community seeing the value in Jesus' power to restore broken lives, it reacts towards him with great fear.

- Fear causes us to suffer muscle failure in our moral courage.
- Fear is the crippling disease that leaves the face of compassion twisted and deformed.
- Fear is the reckless vehicle that crashes into any attempt to show mercy upon those who need it.
- Fear is the opposition party that campaigns to keep courageous compassion from being voted into office.
- Fear is the contractor who continues to build barriers and walls between people groups that prevent them from empathetically "feeling with" one another.
- Fear is the fake optometrist who damages our vision and prevents us from seeing that all humans come from the same sacred womb of God, therefore making us all brothers and sisters.

The community's fear prevents it from seeing Jesus' ability to change this man's life as a positive, faith-based initiative. Jesus' courageous compassion could bring about personal renewal in their cities and towns among other people living in cemetery conditions.

Jesus' critics may not believe in him, but at least they can make the admission that he does seem to bring about a personal change in the lives of those who put their faith in him. The wise founding fathers of our modern democracy saw the wisdom in not banishing the practice of this belief from the American public square. Mark the evangelist wants the reader to understand that Jesus is able to bring about a spiritual recalibration in the lives of people. He is also able to bring peace among people groups, enabling them to live in harmony and moving them from the brink of chaos to the blessing of community. Despite how communities negatively react to those who change the world in good ways, we will not lose hope. Our vision of a spiritually healthy world is not blurred by humankind's irrational global behavior.

- I still choose to believe that courageous compassion is our strength that allows us to confront and change what is ugly in our world.
- I still believe that courageous compassion is what is required for the healing of the nations.
- I still believe that courageous compassion is the great slayer of injustice.
- I believe that the world that seems so irrational will one day be bound, tamed, subdued, and seated at the feet of the Compassionate One who rules the heavens and the earth.

Our vision inspires us to go into the entire world, viewing it with great optimism because the Compassionate One lives. We have a great story to share with our loved ones. We can tell them about the great things the Compassionate One has done for us. Let us celebrate the healing presence that is still in our world. I know that we have much to tell about the working of God in our lives.

Because the man is now set free, he has something to offer to his community and to his society. He wants to follow Jesus, but Jesus tells him no. Instead, he sends him back to tell his family and friends about the great compassionate mercy he received. We too must tell the story about how courageous compassion changed our own lives. I'm sure we all have a story to share about our time in the cemetery.

If anyone ever doubted the ability to experience personal change, then this man's experience should settle the question. If he can be changed from being a demon-possessed, graveyard-dwelling lunatic into an orderly, self-controlled person sitting, dressed, and in his right mind, there is hope for everyone.

9

The Spirit of Independence

Compositional Notes

I delivered this message on July 4, 2010 at the Highland Church of Christ in Abilene, Texas. My family and I regularly worship with Highland and this sermon was presented while I was doing interim preaching with the congregation.

My intention at the outset of this sermon is to identify the underlying fear that influences the interactions of racial groups in America. Exodus 1:9 provides the language to describe the dominant group's fear of falling to minority status.

- It speaks to the fear the oppressor lives with each day.
- It is the fear that the slave will one day grow to rule over the master.

- It is the fear that once the slave ascends to power, he will rule over the master with an intense spirit of retribution.
- It is the haunting fear of racial revenge.

This verse provides the sermon a window through which the audience can see the disastrous consequences of racial fear. Racial fear prompts the dominant group to protect itself from extinction by any means necessary. Pharaoh leads the dominant group in Egypt to create an environment designed to bring about the extinction of the cultural group it perceives as a threat.

In Exodus 1:15 we are introduced to the spirit of independence. Shiphrah and Puah are two Hebrew women enlisted by the king to murder the Hebrew male children. They refused to follow the king's fear based edict. As a result of their spirit of independence they are highly esteemed before today's audience, exalted as an example of the need for Christians to refuse to follow any command to hate or to kill others in the name of racial protection.

Pharaoh's obsession with numbers makes it possible for me to touch on the rising anxiety in this country concerning how racial groups will be counted in the 2010 and 2020 census. Racial groups in this country are competing for numerical status and resources. I seek to persuade Christians to be mindful that such a climate of fear-based racial competition can drive us to a state of genocide. I rely heavily upon the book written by Paul Rusesabagina to make this point.[1] Rusesabagina details the horrible experience of the genocide in Rwanda in 1994 where over 800,000 people were killed. Prior to genocide, both Rwanda and Nazi Germany were considered to be "Christian nations"!

THE SPIRIT OF INDEPENDENCE

Exodus 1:6-22

In Exodus 1:6 we are introduced to a minority group in Egypt that is experiencing an explosive birth rate. It is growing so fast that its number is about to surpass that of the majority population. Exodus reports, "The Israelites were fruitful and multiplied greatly and became exceedingly numerous, so that the land was filled *with them*."

The Hebrew minority had come a long way since their first ancestor, Joseph, arrived in Egypt as a slave. Despite Joseph's status as a slave, his dedication to God resulted in his exaltation to a position of great power in Egypt. Joseph served the Egyptian empire with exceptional distinction. His influence with Pharaoh benefited his descendants and enabled their advancement and progress in the nation.

However, according to Exodus 1:8, a new king came to power who was unaware of how the Hebrews' ancestor had contributed to the greatness and advancement of the Egyptian empire. The new king's main agenda was to curtail the explosive birth rate among the Hebrew minority.

Pharaoh says to the Egyptians, "The Israelites have become much too numerous for us. Come, we must deal shrewdly with them or they will become even more numerous and, if war breaks out, will join our enemies, fight against us and leave the country." It amazes me how a change in a nation's governmental administration can overnight change a nation's attitude, for good or ill, towards a targeted minority group in its midst.

Though the Israelites had been in Egypt for many years, they were still viewed as ethnic outsiders. The Hebrew people were "in" Egypt but were not viewed as being "of" Egypt. This is evident from the king's language. He says, "Come, *we* must deal shrewdly with *them* or *they* will become even more numerous and, if war breaks out, will join *our* enemies, fight against *us* and leave the country."

This language sounds familiar to today's American discourse regarding the Hispanic community. American political interests have monitored the rapid growth of the Hispanic community over the past thirty years in the United States. In the minds of skillful politicians in both parties, huge numbers among Hispanics represent a large voting bloc.

In some instances both major political parties in America have dealt shrewdly with the Hispanic community in regards to immigration reform. For example, the Republican Party will oppose immigration reform if it perceives that the Hispanic community is unquestioningly loyal to the political platform and economic agenda of the Democratic Party, and vice versa. Under President George W. Bush, Democrats feared Hispanics would join the Republican Party. Today, under President Barack Obama, Republicans fear that the largest minority in America will cast its lot with the Democratic Party.

While political chess is being played with the Hispanic community, the fear profiteers use their media outlets to paint a scary picture in the mind of the majority population. They predict what will happen if America's two largest minority groups join forces under the tent of the Democratic Party. Fear mongers appear to be successfully programming the majority population to vote a certain way. Many today approach the voting booth with the intention of not voting according to their moral conscience but to preserve their racial dominance in America.

With these major numerical shifts and political alliances taking place in America it is understandable why the majority population is feeling an increased anxiety. With the continued trend of growth in the minority populations in this country it is predicted that the skin on Mrs. Liberty's face will inevitably have a darker pigmentation by the year 2050.

There is no greater example of the racial fear that accompanies the changing racial reality in America than in Richard D. Fuerle's *Erectus*

Walks Amongst Us.[2] Mr. Fuerle says: "When the environment changes, behavior that was so adaptive that it made a population supreme may be so maladaptive that it leads them towards extinction. Such is the case with whites, whose intra-group cooperation and altruism took them to the top, but now that they are no longer isolated from other races, their altruism is their Achilles' heel, leaving them a mere resource to be used by others. Yet changing their innate, now maladaptive, behavior may be more difficult for them than watching their race disappear forever."

Fuerle's comments provide evidence that racial competition forces group members to keep the racial purity of their group's bloodline intact. The purist agenda makes it increasingly difficult for there to be any genuine racial mixing. The constitution of each racial group is written in the separatist language of "us" and "ours" versus "them" and "theirs."

We are shown in Exodus 1:11-14 that the "us" versus "them" mentality caused the Egyptians to put slave masters over the Israelites to oppress them with forced labor. "But the more they were oppressed the more they multiplied and spread; so the Egyptians came to dread the Israelites and worked them ruthlessly. They made their lives bitter with hard labor in brick and mortar and with all kinds of work in the fields; in all their hard labor the Egyptians used them ruthlessly."

No matter how brutal the oppression, it was unable to disrupt the numerical growth of the Israelites. Therefore the king decides to employ a more inhumane method to abort the accelerated birth rate among the Israelites. The king signs into law a policy that authorizes the murder of male Hebrew infants. He takes this extreme measure in order to secure the Egyptians' ethnic dominance in Egypt.

Some claim that the same is true today. Among America's largest minority groups, males are most likely to have the worst statistics stacked against them when it comes to education, unemployment, health, crime, and prison. Did you know that black men live seven fewer years than males in other racial groups?[3]

Courageous Compassion

The king instructs the Hebrew midwives, Shiphrah and Puah, to murder innocent children. Fear makes people do unthinkable things to other human beings. Pharaoh's arrogance and sense of royal entitlement cause him to expect Shiphrah and Puah to participate in the destruction of an ethnic group to alleviate what he perceives as a potential threat to his people's numeric dominance. Pharaoh says, "When you help the Hebrew women in childbirth and observe them on the delivery stool, if it is a boy, kill him; but if it is a girl, let her live."

What will Shiphrah and Puah do? Are they going to go along with this senseless killing and hide behind the belief that they are exempt from such a murderous deed because they are simply "following orders"?

In Exodus 1:17 courage steps forth and announces the grand entrance of Shiphrah's and Puah's brave spirit. These two Hebrew midwives feared God and did not do what the king of Egypt had told them to do; they let the boys live. It is said that God was kind to the midwives and the people increased and became even more numerous. And because the midwives feared God he gave them families of their own. God honors Shiphrah and Puah. They stand forth as shining examples of what it means to defy a despotic leader's orders to kill.

When Pharaoh realizes that he cannot get Shiphrah and Puah to cooperate in destroying the targeted minority, he then turns to his own people. He uses the royal power of his office to order the majority population to kill minority male children. Pharaoh says, "Every boy that is born you must throw into the Nile, but let every girl live." At least Pharaoh did not force the Hebrew women to have abortions. He simply wanted them killed once they were out of the womb!

There exists today a moral contradiction in the people who, on the one hand, vehemently preach against abortion, but on the other hand, want to cut all government support designed to prolong the child's life after it has been born. The active killing of unborn babies is no more immoral than the passive neglect of the needs of children after they have been born!

It is in light of this Exodus story that I especially appeal to you my white brothers and sisters who have named the name of Jesus Christ. If the earthly kings of talk radio such as Mike Savage, Rush Limbaugh, or G. Gordon Liddy ever issue an edict in coded language to kill others in the name of a violent overthrow of the federal government, I pray you will express the independent spirit of Shiphrah and Puah.

Some politicians like Governor Rick Perry of Texas are flirting with the idea of Texas possibly succeeding from the union.[4] There are vocal politicians in the Tea Party movement who are even more vocal than the governor of Texas. Some radio voices are openly inciting the masses to seriously consider armed resistance against what is perceived as an invasive government. Such rhetoric is disturbing because a close study of history reminds us that genocides and ethnic cleansings often erupt under the cover of a "civil war."

We as a nation would be wise to pay serious attention to Paul Rusesabagina's description of how politicians used the medium of radio and the talent of certain radio personalities to create the hateful climate that preceded the awful outbreak of civil war and genocide in Rwanda in 1994. Within a few months 800,000 Tutsis had been killed. Paul Rusesabagina is the actual person whose life is portrayed in the movie "Hotel Rwanda."

Rusesabagina says, "As the winter faded into the new year of 1994, the talk on the radio grew bolder and louder. Listeners couldn't help but notice that almost every broadcast seemed to feature an over arching narrative. And that story was that the country was in danger from an internal threat and the only solution was to fight that threat with any means necessary." We are mistaken if we think that genocide is a phenomenon confined to Africa.

Rusesabagina makes a keen observation about genocides when he says "it has happened in every culture on the planet, in every period, and the advancement of civilization has been no protection. The same nation that gave us Goethe and Beethoven also gave us Hitler. There will be others, and perhaps some in unexpected locations and the only question will be whether uninvolved people have the courage to take a risk to save strangers."

There may come a time when the white majority in America is encouraged by racist ideologues to actively join in the collective genocide of certain ethnic groups that are perceived as threats. I appeal now to white Christians in the name of the Most High God to begin building the inner strength of Shiphrah and Puah. Begin now to say *no* to any and all subliminal messages suggesting that you destroy the lives of other human beings simply because they are not of your race, political party, or religion.

In a time that beckons for racial and ethnic genocide, every Christian should follow the example of Dietrich Bonheoffer and the Confessing Church in Germany. When Adolf Hitler initiated and inspired the reign of merciless killings of millions of Jews, Dietrich Bonheoffer and the Confessing Church expressed a spirit of independence like Shiphrah and Puah by refusing to take part in a heinous act of mass murder.

Let us pray for an outbreak of confessing churches all across America. Let every church confess that the Lordship of Jesus Christ is greater than the lordship of race and ethnic loyalties. Let churches confess today that our salvation is not in our racial identities but our salvation is in our identification with the death, burial, and resurrection of the crucified life of Jesus Christ.

The time has come in the history of our nation for judgment to begin at the House of God. Do our worship assemblies reflect, both racially and culturally, that the church is truly the House of prayer for all nations and all peoples? On the other hand, do our churches in America today continue to be more in tune with the racial and ethnic divisions that exist in the broader culture? It is imperative that Christians never become satisfied with the church being the only place in America that provides a comfortable sanctuary for racial separatism.

Christians can overcome their fear of this world's Pharaoh-like powers and mend the racial rift that exists within the church and beyond. It will take courage to confront the spirit of racial separatism that permeates our pews every Sunday morning. It takes courage for Shiphrah and Puah to "just say no" to Pharaoh.

How was it possible for two Hebrew midwives to prevail against the king of Egypt? We are given the secret to Shiphrah's and Puah's great courage. Exodus 1:20 tells us that Shiphrah and Puah "feared God!" Because they feared God, they had no fear of man! Because they feared God, they exhibited an independent spirit that could not be intimidated by Pharaoh. These brave women refused to endorse the wickedness perpetrated by a cruel and sadistic regime.

Shiphrah and Puah resembled the independent spirit of their ancestor Joseph. We are told in Genesis 39:9 that when Potiphar's wife commanded Joseph to commit adultery with her he refused to do so. Joseph asks Potiphar's wife in Genesis 39:9, "How then could I do such a wicked thing and sin against God?" No doubt, Shiphrah and Puah asked the same question, "How can we do such a wicked thing and sin against God?"

Christians today should ask, "How can we do such a wicked thing and sin against God?"

- How can Christians passively wish for the demise of other people groups that threaten the dominance of their own race?
- How can Christians remain unmoved by the educational needs of children in America who are not a part of the dominant culture?
- How can Christians keep silent in the face of any sinister plan that is designed to deal shrewdly with the global workforce?
- How can Christians look the other way while children from growing minority groups are filling America's prisons like cattle being herded into the slaughter "pen"?

- How can Christians see the incarceration of young men of color as a convenient strategy to prevent the further "browning" of the general population in America?

I earnestly appeal to all Christians in America to place your citizenship in the kingdom of God above all ethnic loyalties. God is in control of the preservation of every ethnic group on the earth. We are the creation of his hands and he decides how long we will be on the earth. God is the divine social engineer. He is the divine census taker.

The spilled blood of Jesus on Calvary made it possible for every race and tongue to cease from playing the numbers game. The good news of the kingdom is now preached to all nations and all peoples of the earth. God's kingdom liberates us from obsessing over the numerical growth of our particular race. The Holy Spirit empowers us to look beyond the 2010 and the 2050 census. Our focus is not on the census taken in the Egypt lands of this world. Our focus is on that heavenly census to be taken in the New Jerusalem.

The heavenly census is the census that John saw on the Isle of Patmos. John said he saw a number that no man could number. It was a number that consisted of peoples from every nation and every tongue on the earth. That's the number that motivates us!

Endnotes

Introduction

1. President Barack Obama explained in a statement released on June 19, 2009, http://www.juneteenth.com/whitehouse.htm. Gordon's announcement came more than two months after Lee's surrender and the end of the Civil War. "Those who found themselves still enslaved in Galveston had their hopes realized and their prayers answered," President Obama noted. Because of the Galveston proclamation, June 19th is now an official holiday in thirty-one states and celebrated annually.
2. Quoted in E. W. Kenworthy, "Civil Rights Bill Passed, 73-27; Johnson Urges All to Comply; Dirksen Berates Goldwater," *New York Times*, June 20, 1964, A1.
3. This quote and those in the following three paragraphs are from: Kenworthy, "Civil Rights Bill Passed," *New York Times*, June 20, 1964, A1.
4. Kenworthy, "Civil Rights Bill Passed," *New York Times*, June 20, 1964, A1.
5. Carl Spain, "Modern Challenges to Christian Morals," *Abilene Christian College Lectures 1960* (Abilene, Tex.: Abilene Christian College Students Exchange, 1960), 217.
6. Ibid.
7. The history of *Brown v. Board of Education* argues that the carrot is more effective than the stick in effecting compliance with legal decisions that require massive changes in the behavior of large numbers of people. See Kenneth M. Holland, "Compliance with Brown v. Board of Education: The Role of the Elementary and Secondary Education Act of 1965," Benjamin L. Hooks Symposium: "*America's Second Revolution: The Path to and from* Brown v. Board of Education," March 12-14, 2004, Memphis, Tennessee., 26. See also, Christine H. Rossell, *The Carrot or the Stick for School Desegregation Policy: Magnet Schools or Forced Busing* (Philadelphia: Temple University Press, 1990), and James T. Patterson, *Brown v. Board of Education: A Civil Rights Milestone and Its Troubled Legacy* (New York: Oxford University Press, 2001).
8. Richard Hughes, *Reviving the Ancient Faith: The Story of Churches of Christ in America* (Grand Rapids, Mich.: Eerdmans, 1996), 290.
9. Quoted in the Charleston, *West Virginia Gazette*, http://www.wvgazette.com/News/200805190255.
10. Eleven years later, news of the apology continues to appear on the ACU webpage: http://www.acu.edu/events/news/991122-apology.html.
11. Hughes, 297.
12. Spain, 216.
13. Ibid., 218-219.
14. Unknown author. Marginal comments, Spain, 217, in possession of the author.

15 The Glenn Beck radio show (www.therightscoop.com), March 2, 2010. Available on YouTube at: http://www.youtube.com/watch?v=5c4DqdleJuY&feature=related
16 Luke 4:16-19.
17 Acts 4:34-35. Jesus' entire ministry was prophetically anticipated by Mary who declared, "He hath put down the mighty from their seats, and exalted them of low degree. He hath filled the hungry with good things; and the rich he hath sent empty away" (Luke 1:52-53, KJV).
18 These three phrases, all noting Scripture's emphasis on paradigmatic issues, come from the Gospels (Matthew 22:34-40; 23:23) and Paul (I Corinthians 15:3).
19 Amos 5:24, NASV.
20 I am grateful to Lee C. Camp for his memory of this observation from ACU Old Testament Professor, John T. Willis.

Chapter 1

1 *Parrhesia*, translated as bold, free, or candid speech, is ascribed to Peter and John in Acts 4, whose "bold speech" astonished the members of the Sanhedrin when the two apostles were brought before that governing body to answer for their preaching (v. 13). It is the quality that the believers later pray for in response to this first resistance to the preaching of the gospel ("...enable your servants to speak your word with great boldness," 4:29); finally, it characterizes the Acts account of God's answer to their prayer: "And they were all filled with the Holy Spirit and spoke the word of God boldly" (4:31). Cornell West describes *parrhesia* as "fearless speech . . . that unsettles, unnerves, and unhouses people from their critical sleepwalking." He points to Socrates as the model of *parrhesia*, whose "courageous opposition to the seductive yet nihilistic sophists of his day—Greek teachers who employed clever but fallacious arguments—exposed the specious reasoning that legitimated their quest for power and might." *Democracy Matters: Winning the Fight Against Imperialism* (New York: Penguin Press, 2004), 16. For an extended treatment of *parrhesia* as a philosophical and rhetorical construct, see Michel Foucault and Joseph Pearson, *Fearless speech* (Los Angeles: Semiotext(e), 2001).
2 As the forgoing analysis will show, Taylor's evolving construction of the position of the audience turns on what Kenneth Burke viewed as the essence of rhetoric, identification, through which separate individuals experience a sense of being joined together or, as Burke put it, "consubstantial," sharing "common sensations, concepts, images, ideas, or attitudes." Burke recognized that this identification might be rhetorically created through the suggestion of a shared principle or interest, or in opposition to a common enemy, or through more subliminal processes such as when one would "praise God . . . in terms that happen also to sanction one system of material property rather than another." He also notes the power of particular forms or structures of arrangement within discourse to create a sense of identification; by "collaborating" with the form, the audience experiences identification with the content presented in the form as well as with each other. See *Rhetoric of Motives* (Berkeley: University of California Press, 1969), 20-27, 55-59.

3   Accounts of black preaching typically emphasize the fact that the African American sermon is a performative and communal genre of discourse. In other words, in the African American tradition, the sermon truly comes into existence only in the moment of its oral performance, when theological ideas come alive in the preacher's voice and body. The African American sermon is also a communal event, one that results from a process of co-creation involving both preacher and congregation—a feature most obvious in such traditional elements of the sermon as the call and response. As I have argued elsewhere, black preaching is also mimetic, in the sense that sermons do far more than explain or argue in an effort to win the audience's assent to particular theological propositions. Instead, preacher and congregation together use language, sound, and movement to create a shared experience of those propositions. Whereas in many Western homiletic and rhetorical traditions the audience stands removed from the sermon's content, hearing *about* it and rationally evaluating it from "the outside," the black sermon places hearers subjectively "in" the content, so that they imaginatively experience its veracity. For this reason, the foregoing analysis will be based on a recording of the sermon. All quotations are from my transcription of the actual performance. For a rhetorical account of black preaching generally, see G. Selby, "Preaching as Mimesis: The Rhetoric of the African American Sermon," in *And the Word Became Flesh: Studies in History, Communication, and Scripture in Memory of Michael W. Casey*, edited by Thomas H. Olbricht and David Fleer (Eugene, Ore.: Pickwick Publications, 2009), 247-65. Standard accounts of black preaching include: Bruce A. Rosenberg, *Can These Bones Live? The Art of the American Folk Preacher* (1970; rev. ed., Urbana, Ill.: University of Chicago Press, 1988); Gerald L. Davis, *I got the Word in me and I can sing it, you know: A study of the Performed African-American Sermon* (Philadelphia: University of Pennsylvania Press, 1985); Henry H. Mitchell, *Black Preaching: The Recovery of a Powerful Art* (Nashville: Abingdon Press, 1990); E. Crawford, *The Hum: Call and Response in African American Preaching* (Nashville: Abingdon Press, 1995); Cleophus J. LaRue, *The Heart of Black Preaching* (Louisville: Westminster John Knox Press, 2000); and Theresa L. Fry Brown, *Weary Throats and New Songs: Black Women Proclaiming God's Word* (Nashville: Abingdon Press, 2003).
4   Quoted in Richard Lischer, *The Preacher King: Martin Luther King, Jr., and the Word that Moved America* (New York: Oxford, 1995), 138-39.
5   Mitchell, 119-22.

Chapter 9

1   Paul Rusesabagina with Tom Zoellner, *An Ordinary Man: The True Story Behind Hotel Rwanda* (London: Bloomsbury Publishing, 2006).
2   The book in its entirety is online at http://erectuswalksamongst.us/.
3   This statistic is found online at http://menshealth.about.com/od/blackhealth/a/Af_amer_stats.htm
4   See http://www.statesman.com/news/content/region/legislature/stories/04/17/0417gop.html.

ALSO AVAILABLE

Preaching Character

Reclaiming Wisdom's Paradigmatic Imagination for Transformation

Essays and sermons by

DAVID FLEER, JERRY TAYLOR, THOMAS G. LONG,
SCOT MCKNIGHT, ALYCE MCKENZIE, SALLY BROWN, AND OTHERS

"Bland and Fleer range over Scripture like a deer in the forest panting after living water. Here they have gathered at the watering hole of Scripture with an impressive assemblage of preachers, scholars, and interpreters. We are invited to drink deeply with them from texts of wisdom. The focus on wisdom is a welcome one; the wisdom texts provide a serious counter to the frantic ideologies among us (inviting a deep breath of reflection), and an alternative to the technical reason among us that reduces everything to thin knowledge and control. The outcome is a volume of shrewd, nuanced introduction that teems with rich access points into this neglected part of Scripture."

—Walter Brueggemann,
author of *An Unsettling God: The Heart of the Hebrew Bible*

Trade paper $22.99
ISBN 978-0-89112-544-0
252 pages

"Fleer and Bland have done it again! This rich collection of essays and sermons not only offers the Wisdom Literature as an important and exciting source for preaching, but also reaffirms the role of preaching in forming faithful character."

—Charles L. Campbell,
Duke Divinity School; author of *The Word before the Powers: An Ethic of Preaching*

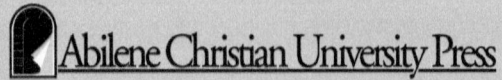

877-816-4455 order toll free
www.abilenechristianuniversitypress.com

www.ingramcontent.com/pod-product-compliance
Lightning Source LLC
Chambersburg PA
CBHW020654300426
44112CB00007B/376